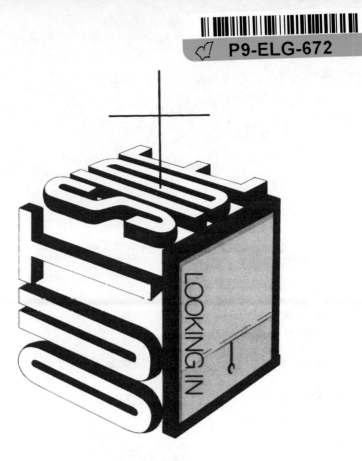

GORDON BRUCE TURNER

FOREWORD BY HENRI J. M. NOUWEN

The United Church Publishing House

The United Church of Canada
Toronto

ISBN 0-919000-37-1

Publisher: R.L. Naylor
Editor: Patricia Clarke

Cover Design and Illustration: Marianne Bird

FOREWORD

After having read Gordon Turner's "Outside Looking In," one sentence from the Gospel of John had gained new strength and new depth for me. It is the well-known verse: "No one can have greater love than to lay down his life for his friends." (John 15:13)

When I first considered these words more than thirty-five years ago, I thought of them in very dramatic terms. "Laying down your life for your friends" then meant considering your life less important than the life of your friends and dying for their sake. I vividly remember how, as a teenager, I wondered whether I would have the courage to let myself be thrown to the lions, burned at the stake or slowly dismembered in defense of my friends. Martyrdom in the most literal way seemed to be what Jesus was asking for.

But as I entered more deeply into the Christian life, was ordained to the priesthood and lived my life in service of Word and Sacrament, I gradually came to see that martyrdom, which literally means witness, requires something much more radical than the heroism of undergoing a violent death. Jesus' words about laying down your life apply to every moment of our existence. They touch the essence of the Christian ministry. They ask of us to let our whole life, our joys and pains, our hopes and doubts, our victories and failures, our ecstasies and agonies, yes, every part of our struggle to live righteous lives, become part of our ministry to others. Ministry in its deepest meaning is martyrdom, witnessing with our whole being to God's faithfulness in our individual and communal lives.

Gordon Turner's book makes this point in a very convincing way. With many concrete and deeply moving examples, he shows that Evangelization and Pastoral Care can never be separated. To think, speak or act as if the ministry of the evangelist is diametrically opposed to the ministry of the caring pastor, does harm to the work of evangelism as well as to the work of pastoral care. Gordon Turner says it very explicitly: "All ministry is — or ought to be — pastoral care. That was the way I was reared in ministry. I see no reason in mature years to change that perception."

In his care-filled study about Evangelization, Gordon Turner makes it very clear that only through deep personal caring can true Evangelization take place. For Evangelization to be non-manipulative, non-pushy and non-possessive, it needs to be a form of witness that is based on the personal faith experience of those who proclaim the Good News of Jesus.

I am aware what a tough challenge this book offers. It is such a temptation to become a professional, a person who evangelizes from a professional distance and who remains outside of the personal struggle. It also is a temptation to self-revealers who think that our personal experience is the only norm and that telling our most intimate story will by itself bring people closer to God. "Laying down your life for your friends" is the hard challenge of the Christian witness, in which we allow our own lives to be given to others in such a way that they find not us, but the One who calls them to conversion and a new life.

This hard task of ministry, in which pastoral care and evangelization are never separated, cannot be accomplished outside of the Christian community. As long as Christian Witness is seen primarily as a heroic task of individual people, we will always be tempted to become distant professionals or sentimental self-revealers. Gordon Turner illustrates very beautifully that the Witness of the individual Christian can only be fruitful in the context of the Christian community. No Christians can minister unless the community calls and sends them. In that sense, the Church is the evangelist as well as the caregiver even when the ministry is exercised by its individual members. Gordon Turner writes: "the future of the Church as evangelist lies in its ability to become the community of the walking wounded." For me, this means a community of people

iv

who are willing to lay down their lives, individually while living in community, for their brothers and sisters who search for a new sense of belonging to God and each other.

I am grateful for this book. It is a book that creates unity by bridging false gaps in the ministry, and preventing unnecessary divisions. It brings us back to the truth that all true ministry is martyrdom. Gordon Turner has not hesitated to offer his own struggles in the ministry as the way to open for us this perspective. His willingness to lay down his own life for his friends, and then to do, in this book, what he speaks about, makes him a very convincing and hope-giving witness of the Lord Jesus Christ.

HENRI J.M. NOUWEN

IN MEMORY OF

SEWARD HILTNER, A.B., Ph.D.,
Professor of Theology and Personality
Princeton Theological Seminary

"A friend and advisor who kept me going."

AND FOR

WILLIAM E. "MOE" ROBINSON, M.D., C.M.,
C.R.C.P.(C)
Pschoanalyst and Teacher

"A wounded healer, advisor, and friend
who keeps me going."

TO BOTH

WITH THANKS AND GRATITUDE
FOR SHARING MY JOURNEY IN LIFE!

Table of Contents

OUTSIDE LOOKING IN

INTRODUCTION

"Anybody seen Grace Brown lately?"

Listening! I listened deeply, in the early days in my third parish, to discover the basic concerns of its people. The early stories one hears among one's new parishioners often tell the deepest truths of their concerns and hopes as a people of God.

That was the way it was at Harmony United Church. Someone would ask with nostalgic wistfulness: "I wonder whatever happened to Grace Brown? She used to be so active here. She headed the women's organization and was always at the turkey supper. She was one of the first women elders we ever had. Marvelous woman. But now we never see her anymore. I wonder what happened?"

Later that week the question would be put by another wistful church historian. "You would have liked Bill Smith. Super guy. And real helpful around this church. That gymnasium beside the church, he built it almost single-handedly. But you never see him around any more. I think it's been about six years. Not even for Christmas now. I wonder what happened to Bill Smith?"

It wouldn't be so bad if there had been just a few Bill Smiths and Grace Browns in the life of that church. However, we soon found out there were dozens, even hundreds, who had come through the front doors of our suburban church, moved into its worship and life of that suburban church, and then slipped out unnoticed — or at least not noticeably engaged with — through the back door.

Harmony had begun as a small rural church. The original worship centre was in the farm house on the property purchased for its future. That farm house was still there in 1972 when I became pastor. The stories about it were many and powerful. Later a gymnasium was attached to the farm house. It was not exactly a thing of beauty, but it housed beautiful people who dared to dream. In the 1960s, like many other congregations, they decided to build a new and large sanctuary. It would seat 700 persons because the east end of the city, which had encroached on this little country community, was scheduled to "boom". Well, it didn't. At least not on schedule.

Attendance at Harmony always seemed to be about the same throughout this period. It was a vital, medium sized church. About 200 would turn out on any given Sunday — a pretty meagre crowd for that big a building.

People didn't notice another factor. While the number of active members remained about the same, a good many folk kept coming into the church. Confirmation classes were a reasonable size. Baptisms were celebrated. Young families were apparent everywhere. People were coming into the church — but they were also going at about the same rate. And nobody seemed to notice. Certainly nobody did anything about it.

Harmony Church is not unique. Nobody seems to notice in any church. People come and people go. We don't notice. Or if we do, we do nothing about it. We have an awesome back door syndrome in our churches. At least, that is what the stories of the church dropouts whom I have interviewed seem to tell me.

In the decade of the 1960s The United Church of Canada lost 10 per cent of its adult confirmed members. That's bad news! What is sucking them out of the life of the church? The only good news is that every other mainline denomination in North America suffered a similar decline. It has become known as the 10 percent decline decade.

Thousands of former church members are on the outside looking in. They were once part of the life and witness of

2

the church; they are now members of the hurt or indifferent mass who look at the church with bitter memory.

What can one do about these people on the outside looking in? What might help them re-engage with their faith journey, that is, if they wanted to? Could Bill Smith and Grace Brown be encouraged to give the church a second look?

In 1978 I took my first stab at finding out. I was looking for a test population for a doctoral thesis project in "pastoral conversation". I remembered the early stories I had heard at Harmony about the Browns and Smiths. I had met many like them during six years in that community. Because of their anger toward the church, I thought they might make an interesting group on which to test some new ideas on the nature of pastoral care techniques.

The original typology was developed in the Harmony Church congregation. The stores of the persons interviewed, whether in the original research or later, have been significantly altered in order to protect their confidentiality. All the stories are told as if they happened in the life of that one parish, as if these persons were all once associated with a particular church located in time and space in suburban Oshawa. Hence, Harmony Church has become our global congregation in a somewhat global village. It may be, for you, your church in your town or city.

What I didn't bargain for, however, was that this would become a transforming experience for my ministry. I began to discover that a pastoral theologian was moving out of his chosen field into the area of evangelization. Horrors! I had never liked the word "evangelism". And here it was the thing I was doing.

Now I find myself an evangelism executive. These years have been among the most exciting in my ministry. I'm at the centre of the most exciting mandate the church has — inviting persons to consider the invitation to be citizens in the Commonwealth of God. My transformation in ministry came through those encounters with the church dropouts.

So if there is any credit due for this book, it belongs to the dropouts from that congregation in suburban Oshawa, Ontario, Canada. Great folk they were, and good friends many of them are — some inside and some outside the church now.

3

Also credit is due to the many dozens of other church dropouts I have since interviewed in our Congregational Renewal Clinics and in streets, restaurants and pubs of Canadian cities. Still others I have heard of from participants in my clinics throughout Canada, the USA, New Zealand and Australia. To them all I say, "Thank you for sharing your stories." I have learned much from them. They have made my ministry more meaningful and substantial.

I would also like to express a debt to the people of that Harmony United Church congregation. They are one of the great churches in this land. At least, they are great to me. You might visit them and sense very ordinary Christian folk. But you never find the pearl until you break open the shell. Some of the greatest Christian persons I've met come through the doors of 15 Harmony Road North on Sundays. Harmony is not just the street address. It represents the spiritual tenor of a group committed to the journey in Christ. The people of Harmony made that journey with me. They even encouraged me on it. When it became confession time for their past actions as a church, they understood that one of the moments of confession was repentance, and that meant changed behaviour.

Ask the church dropouts in their midst. You know, those who were on the outside looking in and are now on the inside looking out. The people of Harmony learned some lessons about their future in ministry. They, too, were my teachers. They continue to be a model for me about what the church can become.

Since leaving the parish to work on the national staff of our church, I have led 50 or more clinics on "pastoral conversation with the church dropout". The members of those clinics have told stories which confirmed the original basis of my data. Often one has been a former dropout. When they have risked in sharing their stories, I have taken particular notice.

Hence the story base of this data now numbers conversations with over 100 of those who are on the outside looking in. To them I express my thanks.

Two persons, in particular, have encouraged me in this journey. The late Seward Hiltner, professor of theology and personality at Princeton Theological Seminary, shepherded me through the original hundreds of pages of recorded verbatim interviews. He was a demanding taskmaster, but a kind friend. He taught me never to be satisfied with the superficial. This book is dedicated to the memory of our sometimes stormy encounters and his words, "You can do better than that, boy."

There is another friend who stands on the outside looking in... an unlikely person to struggle through all the text of understanding how to deal with the church dropout. Not really. His name is Moe Robinson, M.D. His vocation in that of a psychoanalyst and he teaches at the University of Toronto. He taught me most of what I own of self understanding. Indeed he helped me long ago not to become a church dropout. To this good friend I express my heartfelt thanks for the "courage to become".

Although I must accept full and final responsibility for the research and writing of this book, it has become immeasurably more that it otherwise could have because of five persons who have read the last two drafts. Shirley Morrison, who recently died, was a lay person in the Harmony congregation, as is Lloyd Hanna. They were part of the panel of peers for the original doctoral research and they agreed to relisten to this material and other stories of the church dropout for this book. Shirley was a homemaker and Lloyd a business executive and lay chaplain at the local hospital.

Carolyn McKillop is a contributing editor with The United Church Observer and has served as one of the resource persons on a Ventures in Evangelism team. As such she has led clinics based on this research for the past five years.

Lynda Diane McNeil is a teacher with exceptional children in the public school system in Oshawa, who writes church and educational curricula, and has a particular gift for hearing the soft underbelly of human stories. Her specialty is in the area of story-telling and, as a special friend, she has listened caringly to the pain and turmoil of the birthing of this book.

It's not very often — and it's sometimes frightening — when an eminent theologian turns your way and says, "Turner, I'd like to read your manuscript before it sees the light of day." Dr. Brian Fraser of the Vancouver School of Theology really wanted to be helpful, and he was.

Finally, a word of appreciation to Barbara Scott, my secretary and associate in the work of evangelism for some six years. She worked overtime in the encouragement department and made some very helpful suggestions. To all these I say, Thanks for sharing the journey with me.

As I was completing the manuscript for publication, I discovered that Henri Nouwen had moved to live with the L'Arche Community three miles from my doorstep. I had heard much about him from our mutual friend Seward Hiltner. I had read most of his books. He was a spiritual mentor for my journey, albeit at a distance. Since Hiltner had agreed before his death to write the foreword for this book, and since Henri and I had both studied with him, I thought I would chance an invitation to him to do it instead. I am delighted that he agreed.

GORDON BRUCE TURNER
TORONTO, ONTARIO, CANADA.

PART I.
DROPPING OUT

CHAPTER I
ONE COMMON PAINFUL STORY

They were sceptical as they opened the doorway just enough for us to see each other. My introduction as their minister, whom they had never met, didn't meet with open enthusiasm. I indicated that I wanted to talk with people who had formerly been active in the life of our church. Reluctantly they agreed to give me a few moments. That turned out to be the beginning of one of the most creative pastoral relationships I have ever had. For them it was the beginning of walking the road of faith again.

Their story is not unique.

Seventeen years before, their son had died. It was a sudden death. They had turned to the church, and rightly expected its resources to buoy them over this supreme shock in life's journey. The church failed them. Both their pastor and their fellow members in the household of faith were absent. Slowly but surely they moved from the centre of the church, to the fringe, and then out.

Their story went like this. Early one evening their younger son went to the bedroom he shared with his older brother. An hour or so later the older brother went to do his homework and found his younger brother almost unconscious. The young boy was rushed to hospital where, within the hour, he was in a coma. The family was told that his condition was serious. The lad remained in a coma for five days. The pastor did not visit. Few persons from the parish came by, except for close neighbours.

On evening the father called the pastor. He asked him to meet them the next morning at the hospital for family prayer. "I just thought it might help us hang in if Pastor Smythe could say a prayer with us. We were raised Baptist and prayer means a lot to us. It still does." The pastor did visit the hospital the next day. He said a prayer. The parents could remember it almost verbatim.

Perhaps they remember that prayer so well, because it was one of the last moments in which they shared life on this earth with their young son. Life has a way of etching things in our memories at crucial moments. Ron (not his real name) died later that afternoon.

The family made its way home. They looked to their pastor and God for help. Where else can you look at a time like that? Except into the jaws of bitterness and despair! Their pastor kept company with them through the next hours of planning. He took the funeral. It had a special meaning as it was in the church in which the lad had been confirmed into the Christian faith just four months before. Easter time, I think they said. The women of the church held a reception in the church basement for friends and family afterwards. They said it would make it easier. The family could just invite the special few, whom it was easier to cry with, back to their home afterwards. The women of that church have always been like that, considerate and thoughtful.

Those special friends left later that night. The pastor left. And the Banyon family were all alone. All too alone! No one ever came back to share their grief. No one shared their pain and sorrow. They walked the valley of the shadow alone. No shepherd. Only lost lambs.

Yes, you have it right. The pastor never came back again into their home. No other members of the church came in intentional ministry either. No one talked about their son to them.

But you know how it is. We don't like to talk about death and bereavement. Oh, yes, the neighbours leaned over the back fence and asked, "How's it going?" But when the talk shifted to their pain, the neighbours got going. Not easy, this talking about loss and death. And we Christians are no better at it than the rest of the population.

Lest you think I am overly critical of the pastor, let me say a brief word of concern — for him and for the whole church. I have never quite understood why we expect pastors to be all things to all people. Perhaps we have taken Paul's injunction a bit out of context. We expect them to be excellent preachers, super counsellors, adept administrators, superlative pastoral caregivers, and nice folks too — all rolled into one. That's a burden that no one deserves to attempt to shoulder. Yet all too many pastors also expect it of themselves.

All pastors I have worked with have glaring gaps in their garbs of ministry. They do some things excellently, some other aspects of ministry adequately, some poorly, and other essentials badly. Why should we expect every pastor to be able to deal with death in a helpful way? Some of them cannot cope with the possibility of their own demise, just like the rest of us. It is a horrendous experience for them to walk through the door of a funeral parlour. I also know many a doctor who cannot cope with a dying patient. So why should this pastor have been any different?

The Pauline letters talk about the church as a body with many members. Paul also implied that the body would be given all the gifts for ministry that it would need. He didn't say that any one member would be given all the gifts for ministry, but that all members, with their gifts complementing each other, would be adequate for ministry.

Perhaps that's where the church at Harmony failed the Banyon family. If the pastor couldn't, then someone else should have. And could have. He deserves no more of the blame for this church dropout family than any other member of that congregation. We are all ministers of Jesus Christ.

If there is one thesis of this book it is this: we are all evangelizers (good news people); we are all in ministry with the gifts God has entrusted to us. But more of that as we unfold the stories of others. And our own stories.

The Banyons thus began to make the slow journey from the inside of the church towards the outside. It took many months to complete. As they tell it, it was a painful one. They did it reluctantly.

9

The Sunday after Ron's death they were back in the pew where they always sat. A bit lonely and strained; but nonethless they were there. They came back for several Sundays. That was their pattern (which I will refer to later as their church attendance rhythm). After all they had been reared in a fundamentalist Baptist church. One ought to be in church on the Lord's Day. They would be there for four Sundays in a row, then take a day off, to visit relatives perhaps, then back another four Sundays before another absence. That was the pattern for the first four months after Ron's death.

Can you blame the people of Harmony Church? Why should they interfere in the Banyons' private grief? After all, they were doing just fine. They were back at church. "We're so pleased they can deal with a tough situation so well." The pastor too might have assumed that all was well. But it was not!

After four months, their attendance rhythm began to change. Instead of four Sundays in church and one away, it gradually moved to one Sunday there and four away. And after seven months they were never seen in the life of that congregation again.

They slipped out of that church — a mother and a father and their two remaining children — almost unnoticed. No one ever asked why! No one called to encourage them in their life of discipleship. No lay person. No clergyperson. No one.

It would be a sad case of pastoral oversight if it were not so truly typical. No one ever asks the church dropouts why they leave the church. No one hears their cries for help nor sees their tears of sorrow. Yet they leave the church crying and screaming. "S/he who has ears to hear, let them hear what the spirit says to the church."

And so the Banyons left the church. Gone for 17 years before we began our pastoral conversations with them. We'll return to their story in a later chapter.

CHAPTER II
TEARS AND CRIES OF THE JOURNEY

One thing all church dropouts have in common. They all leave the church community in pain. Their stories, without exception, indicate that the journey from the inside to the outside was a painful lonely passage.

John S. Savage, president of Lead Consultants and author of an early work on the church dropout entitled *The Apathetic and Bored Church Member*, once indicated to this writer that all of his interviews with dropouts had been accompanied by emotional overtones.

My own interviews also have always stirred deep emotion. When we get close to the truth about their leaving the church, there are, without exception, tears, tremours in the voice or visible pain. As they rehearse the story for me, they often wonder aloud why others did not notice what was happening in their lives. "I tried to tell them. How blunt do you have to be about it?" "I mean, how blind can some people be?"

The truth is that we are usually blind and deaf to what is happening in the lives of others... and perhaps especially in the caring community known as the church.

"I told the pastor how angry I was when he never went to see my wife in the hospital. But he didn't seem to care! So we just left."

Yes, we are often blind and deaf to the spiritual development or decay in the lives of others. Anger can be heard. Anger can be seen. That is, if we have ears to hear and eyes to see. And if we want to hear "the cries for help" of the church dropout.

Some of them can even be quite explicit. Like getting hit by a truck. Like my friend Anne!

She snarled at me through clenched teeth at the church door after service. "I want to see you tomorrow afternoon."

"Ah, come on! Monday is the pastor's day for liberation. And tomorrow looks like a good day for golf," I said to myself.

But, yes, I was there when she walked into my study, arms loaded with books — Sunday School books — and dropped them in a pile on the floor in front of me. Pretty graphic body language, I'd say. A loud, visual cry for help.

Anne was the lead teacher in our intermediate Sunday School program. Youngsters loved her. She was good at Christian nurture. And here she was quitting... or was she?

As I put my feet up on the desk, I wondered what it all meant. I wondered if the kids were getting to her. Materials too complex? Fed up with every Sunday doing the C.E. thing? Or maybe she missed not being in church with her family — they upstairs and she down in the basement? Wrong on all counts!

After the initial storm, the real story began to unfold. Her father was seriously ill in a distant town. Her immediate family was not able to understand how tough it was on her not to be there. After all, he was an aged man. She was the only daughter and she felt guilty. There were things she needed to say to him before it was too late. However, she had family responsibilities here. She couldn't go to him. Or could she?

An hour or so later she had made some decisions. Surprising to her, the family supported her. They got along all right while she was absent for the next two months. She made her peace with her father. She was there when he died. Anne still is a valued member of the Christian nurture team at Harmony.

You can stop church dropouts in their tracks. Cries for help need to be heard, and acted upon. Church dropouts need not leave the community of the faithful in pain! The church needs to learn some arresting body language of its own. It begins with listening for these cries of help... that lead toward helplessness and hopelessness. They are the beginning of the story of moving from being on the inside looking out to being on the outside looking in.

CHAPTER III
WHO IS A CHURCH DROPOUT?

Perhaps this is a good point at which to begin defining terms. Who are the church dropouts anyway? Are they those who are on the outside of the church, who we assume once had a peripheral touch of the Christian faith? Those who are now ill-at-ease with the christian community? Anyone who is on the fringe of the Christian community? Or merely as the Bible notes, "those who are not for us"?

Current researchers mean a number of things when they refer to the church dropout. My own typology is built around seven factors. Not all of my colleagues would agree with them all. To be a church dropout — a hard core one — I sense that one must touch base with at least five, if not all, of the following seven characteristics.

First, church dropouts 'Never Attend Worship', although they used to be faithful in their attendance. As we say, they have voted with their feet. One of the clearest indicators that persons have become hard core church dropouts is their total lack of being with the Lord's people on the Lord's Day. It is also one of the earliest warning signs.

Second, they are 'Involved in no Church Related Activities. Thus the woman who never attends church but is faithful in her involvement in the church women's group is not technically a dropout. She is still tied to the body of Christ. Dropouts were once involved in activities in vital ways, often in leadership; now, however, they have broken the relationship totally.

Third, 'They Give No Financial Support to the Church',

either locally or nationally. The stewardship of their resources has been directed elsewhere. Often they were people who gave substantially. They now say, in effect, "I'll show them. If they don't need me, they don't need my money either." The persons who make their annual substantial financial donation to their church — but never attend any church related functions including worship — are thus not technically church dropouts. They will tell you that St. George's by-the-Gas-Station is "my church and I give to it".

Fourth, and perhaps the most significant mark, is that they have a 'Negative Attitude to the Church They Used to Attend.' Not just to the Christian church, but to that specific church at the corner where they may have been baptized or married. They speak about that church, old St. George's by-the-Gas-Station. And the heavy intonation pointed at that church makes you know that their attitudes are up to no good about its eternal destiny and worthwhileness!

Fifth, the decision to leave the church was 'Painful'. My research, and conversations with others who have interviewed dropouts, seems to identify a universal principle: church dropouts always leave in pain! It is a pain that they can still feel in conversation with persons who care to listen deeply. It is often hard to go back into the depths of that story again, but it is necessary to do so if they are to be free to re-engage with their once exciting journey of faith.

Surprisingly, a sixth characteristic is that 'They May Often Talk About Faith Issues in a Convincing Way.' So much so that people often mistake them for card carrying attenders. That would not be perceived by them to be a compliment. Of interest, however, is the fact that many of them give evidence of a continuing discipleship outside the church. They tell us that they read their Bibles often and some pray daily and with deep meaning. Their quiet — and private — pietism shames many of us who attend church regularly. It is a continuing mystery why this may be so.

Seventh, and perhaps underlying all of what has been said above, is the fact that they are 'Believers But Not Belongers.' They do not see the need for belonging. The church does not fill the "God-shaped blank" in their lives of which Augustine spoke. They say they still believe in the Christian story but they see no need for affiliation. So they now live 'On The Outside Looking In.'

To summarize then, the marks of identity for the church dropout, as I will be using the term:

1. They never attend worship, but once did on a regular basis.
2. They are involved in no church related activities whatsoever.
3. They give no financial support to the church.
4. They have a negative atttide to the specific church they used to attend.
5. Leaving the church was a painful experience.
6. They may still talk about faith convincingly, and often have a practical pietism.
7. They are believers but not belongers.

Throughout this book we will continue to return time and again to that fifth mark. It is our key to understanding the church dropout. When the church begins to recognize that dropouts do not leave voluntarily but crying and screaming, it begins to grasp the possibilities of reversing the flow.

The truth is that church dropouts don't want to leave. The 'back door syndrome' of the church doesn't have to continue. It is true also that church dropouts can be helped to drop back in. We can become the catalysts for their re-entry.

A local church which continues to be deaf to the cries of its people, however, has begun to plan its funeral service. This is equally true for a denomination which is not ready for radical reform in its training of lay and clergy for ministry. The date of the funeral for both has just not been set!

CHAPTER IV.
THE EBB AND FLOW OF
THE CHURCH DROPOUTS. HOW MANY?

Is it really all that bad, you ask? I mean, really, this church drainage that will see the church's demise is a lot of hyperbole? Right?

I wish it were. The trend of decline indicates that the church could become not just a minority, but an insignificant minority by the year 2000. University of Lethbridge sociologist Reginald Bibby and the Gallup organization in their regular polls indicate the future does not bode well for mainline Protestantism.

Look at the facts! The United Church of Canada, Canada's largest Protestant denomination, peaked in adult confirmed membership in 1965, at 1,064,033. By 1977 its membership had shrunk to 930,226. In 1980 it had 903,302 members and in 1984, adult membership was at a continuing low of 891,384. That shrinkage represented a .1 per cent drop, the lowest of recent date. The most recent figures indicate that the United Church dropped a further 10,000 adult members in 1985, a 1.1 per cent decline rate again. (1) The overall message is that the decline of the 1970s continues. It may be down to a trickle, but in a time of increasing Canadian population we are not even keeping our even.

Most of the major mainline denominations, in Canada and the United States of America, have contributed with equal generosity to the church dropout pool. Most of us continue to decline, albeit more slowly. Nonetheless, the dropout pool affords us all a rich water in which to fish, if we can learn again how we are called to be fishers of humanity. I believe it to be one of the more significant areas for the current focus of evangelization.

Professor Bibby, whose Project Canada is a well documented and significant contribution to the literature of Canadian religious socialization, indicates that those most likely to return to the Christian community are those "so socialized". (2) What Bibby means is that those who have been once in the community of faith have a certain socialized openness to evangelism. They know the Christian story, even if it is but a misty memory. Hence they are easiest to engage again with that story, and to encourage to re-enter the community of the faithful.

There is another reason, however, that I believe the church ought to go fishing in the dropout pond! I believe that dropouts have gifts to give us. Evangelization is not just about what we have to give others — the sharing of our story with them. It is also what others have to give us — yes, the story they have to share with us. By story I mean each one's own perception of what God has been up doing their lives, including their decisions to leave the community of faith. Perhaps as we listen to what their pain-filled journeys have been about, we can learn something about the nature of mission, the failure of the church in that mission, and repentantly, glimpse new meanings for our missiology. I firmly believe that church dropouts have as much to teach us about the potential meaning of the mission of the church as we have to tell them about its mission. Dare we listen to their cries? Might they possibly be a call of God to us?

CHAPTER V.
PROFILES OF THE CANADIAN CHURCH DROPOUT

As I have crossed various continents listening to the stories of church dropouts (as told by them or their friends), I have come to a sense of a collage. The stories I have heard, from the shores of Newfoundland to the tip of Australia, have not appeared to differ significantly. These stories have only heightened my sense of the accuracy of the original research done with the group of dropouts at Harmony Church. Perhaps the painful journeys of the church dropout are more general than most of us imagined.

I had certain hunches about why people leave the church when I began the original research. I sensed that conflict was probably one of the main reasons. When people collide head on with other members of the congregation over some important issue, or when they and the pastor are at variance, they choose either fight or flight. In the church it is generally the latter. It also occurred to me that the increasing secularization of our Canadian culture might leave many without a felt need for the church as a fellowship of witnessing, worshipping and caring people. That is, what do you worship and witness to in this me-generation? Often, you can get all the caring and friendship you need at the golf course or the social club. Who needs the church for that?

Conversations with church dropouts just did not bear out the first hunch. It's more myth than reality that ornery nasty Christians are driving others away. The second hunch, however, was dead on! As a predominant and underlying causative factor, it was largely responsible for many dropout. The good news, however, is that the secularization of religion is not all bad news. There is considerable hope for the secular church living in God's secular world!

In the next chapter I will tell the stories of persons who fall into five specific categories. Under their umbrella, I believe we can cover most of the reasons why people leave the Canadian church. In PART II we will address the curative measures which could help in each of these specific categories. Hence we shall follow the same story lines from PART I to PART II.

The five categories are:
- Inadequate Ministry in Crisis Times
- A Church Not Meeting Personal Needs
- Changes in Life Style
- Conflict with the Pastor or Church Member
- A Crisis of Faith

People leave the church because they received 'Inadequate Ministry in Crisis Times.' People look to the church in their times of need for pastoral care or for "some word from the Lord". When these are found to be wanting, it is a devastating experience. The need-filled person goes away in disillusionment, or more often in anger. People have a right to expect ministry when in pain and need. That, however, is the task of the whole people of God — not of some elect or select caste. Herein lies the historic problem of the church.

When the local church does 'Not Meet Personal Needs' people give the church a deserved yawn! Here we include people whose priorities have changed over the years. The church no longer offers what they feel to be important. Rightly or wrongly, that is how they feel. Others have specific needs, which the church in their experience has been unable to meet. The stories of these folks may have some surprises for us.

Earlier we mention the shift to a predominantly secular society. 'Changes In Life Style' encompass a number of things: leisure society, widowhood, divorce, singleness, gay persons coming out of the closet. When life is changing, can the church, as an institution, change? The stories of dropouts indicate that it does not and maybe cannot!

'Conflict With the Pastor or Another Church Member' was a minor factor, but, as we indicated, not as much as expected. We thus hear something of the why and what of conflict that was unresolved.

Perhaps most interesting to the writer, yet not surprising, was the category of 'A Crisis of Faith'. When people discover that what they believe and what they are doing (or what life is doing to them) are inconsistent, their faith falls apart. It is not an uncommon story. Easier to give up faith than living!

So we move on to listen to their stories. You may want to change their names and places when you find yourself meeting them on Main Street in Your Town.

CHAPTER VI
THE 'WHY' IN WHY THEY LEFT

A. Inadequate Ministry in Crisis Times

You remember the Banyons. We met them in the first chapter. I suspect their story is far more common than we care to admit. Pastors fail persons in crisis times. Church folk fail them as friends. All of us fail each other when we should have been "Christs to each other", as Dietrich Bonhoeffer once called us to be.

Let us listen to another story. Not all crisis times have to do with death, at least physical death, but many of them do have to do with loss of one kind or another. Like Lyla's story.

She returned home late one afternoon after work. The home was unusually quiet. The children were at the park playing, but Jim was usually there with his "Hi Hon, how'd the day go?" But no Jim and no words of greeting. Only a note on the end of the bed and his bedroom closet stripped clean.

She said she had no warning. A marriage counsellor would assess it differently. She said they didn't fight — much. She indicated that she always gave in so that battles wouldn't happen. His note told a different story, however. He had "had it". He didn't want to put up with being "pushed around any more", "being mothered" and told what he "ought to do". He would be in touch in a day or so to work out things. After 25 years of "wedded bliss" (from her perspective), it was all over.

So Lyla, at 48, began a new road in the journey of life. She began the journey in anger and depression. That was natural for a person who had been taken "off guard", or so she told friends. She lashed out at her former husband when he

21

came to see the children. "Why did you do this to us?" She lashed out at her children, often inappropriately. More times than not, she lashed out at friends. And that would make it all the more difficult. They wanted to be good to her, but her anger kept distancing them from her. So many of her nights were spent alone. Her loneliness did not turn into solitude!

In all of this lonely despondent journey, where was the church? Lyla and Jim had been regulars in the life of Harmony Church. He was a member of the Board, she a Martha-type in the women's groups. Lyla went back to church with the youngsters a few Sundays after the split. "You're doggone right I'll keep my head high," she said to friends. "After all, it was Jim who did this to us. My faith is important. Sure I'll keep on with the church." And she did — for several months.

Pastor Gary meanwhile was glad to see her back in the church. She didn't sit in her usual pew. Perhaps it felt a bit uncomfortable. She and the children moved to the other side of the church, a bit further back. He noticed that there were some other single parents who sat there. He was glad she was doing so well. During a visit to her home, about three months after the split, he commented on how well she was doing. He admired people like her who got back to the business of living so easily. It was good for the youngsters too, a good role model of how to handle interpersonal conflict.

But Lyla wasn't doing well. Inside she was crumbling apart. Once she cried for help — though Pastor Gary didn't recognize it as that — when she complained after church about the water stains on the sanctuary wall.

A while later Pastor Gary noticed that Lyla and her family weren't in church. He thought it was about three months since he had seen them. Their visiting elder had missed them too. Perhaps they were going away for weekends. Perhaps we should leave them alone. "You don't want to pry into people's personal lives."

Pastor Gary stood back too. He wondered what might be happening in their lives. He decided that people need to be left alone to their private turmoils. He had called the one time three months after the split. Lyla was doing fine. He never went through her door again. Pastors seldom go through the doors of the church dropouts to ask what's happening.

Lyla and her children soon became hard core dropouts. They spent their Sundays doing other things as a family. They missed church a bit. "But we gave them a chance. They could have helped when we needed it." And the elder never called either. She had once been a single parent and knew the pain of separation; but she had gotten over it herself... and stayed in the church.

B. A Church Not Meeting Personal Needs

The original interviews in the Harmony congregation indicated that the highest percentage of church dropouts left that congregation because it was not meeting their personal needs. It was clear, from these conversations, that these were their needs as they perceived them. Others might find them inappropriate or unrealistic. Nonetheless, some 36 percent of that research population dropped out because the church was not where they were, or was not where they felt the church should be.

They were not generally angry or hostile, more disappointed or indifferent. Today they cross the church threshold only as consumers, for marriages and funerals. Later, we shall note how specific this is for the Anglican communion in the recent research of Reginald Bibby. It has a purely social function to them, dating back to our cultural antiquity.

Like Garth and his delightful younger wife Bett! Their story, I have since confirmed from many other conversations, is a typical Canadian scenario.

Garth and Bett lived in one of the affluent new suburbs outside the Harmony parish area. Both had grown up in the parish, had reared their children through teenaged years there. But luck and effort had blessed them graciously and they had been able to move to the area where people lived who had made it. And certainly Garth had made it economically. He was a well respected member of the business community and president of the Kiwanis club.

Both parents talked fondly of their past in the Harmony

congregation. "We like to get back for the annual turkey supper, you know. Its good to touch base with one's roots. I really like to see old Jimmy and talk about the old days. But, well, we just don't get back to church for anything else now, except that annual pilgrimage. Guess its the same way for a lot of folks."

Their story began to unfold. All of their children had gone to Sunday school and had been confirmed — moments of real pride for Bett and Garth.

Janie, their youngest, seemed to have a particular interest in the church. She was always there and "we wondered if she might even want to work for the church full time. We remember her confirmation well. We were so proud of her. She had made that decision to become part of the church and to take the vows. That was at Easter in 1973. She was in grade 11. That summer we went to the cottage, as we always did. She took her Bible with her, read it a lot, it seemed. Then when we came home that fall we just never did get involved in the church again. Janie went to the teen group for those who had been confirmed. The other two didn't go. And Bett and I, well, we just never did get back at it."

In a later interview the family reflected on why they had never returned to church. "I've always felt that one of the primary roles of the church in society was to help families 'prepare their children for life'. And so when Janie (and the others) had been prepared for life we really had no more need of the church. It wasn't that we had anything against the church, just that we didn't need it any more. I guess you could say we had outgrown it."

So Garth, Bett, and family slipped into the dusk of church life. They had experienced the church as an institution from which they should receive, but not as something through which, or to which, they should give. Once again — and this seems to be the paramount Canadian experience — confirmation had served as graduation out of the church, not as a call to mission within the body of Christ. That is a sad commentary on how we prepare young people for Christian living and how we challenge all people to the ministry of Christ in the world.

Some months after this conversation, I was in their home again when fortuitously two of their children were visiting. Janie was home from Vancouver where she was a nurse, and Bob was on a brief leave from his job as a bush pilot in northern Manitoba. They expressed interest in my project and had heard about my previous visits with their parents. Both indicated that they had not been to church "in years". They also volunteered that they "would probably return to church when they got married and had families of their own". "But as for now, we really have no need of the church... nothing against it, just nothing there for us." Their parting shots in our conversation (to which their parents listened silently) may well have been defensiveness on behalf of their parents. "I guess we'd go back when we had children so they would get properly prepared for life. But then when they were adults, we would probably do as Dad and Mom did and forget about it again."

Three years after this conversation I had an interesting phone call. Janie was coming home to Oshawa to be married. Garth wanted to know if I would be the minister to marry her. "We think of you as our minister now even though we have still not been back to church." Although I was unable to be there because of prior commitments, I did help Garth write the prayer he would give at the wedding banquet. I mention this postscript only to point forward to some later comments we will make about evangelical opportunities for caring ministry with the church dropout.

Not all the stories of church dropouts who claim the church doesn't meet them where they are, are as superficial as that of Garth and Bett. It is easy for us to take their excuses with a grain of salt, to recognize people who are looking for almost any explanation for non involvement. Defensively, we can hardly believe that the claims of the Gospel were so well hidden as not to call out their involvement in ministry in some way. But in their defence we also need to recognize that often the church does ask all too little of its people in terms of discipleship. And, as body builders claim about muscle development, "Use it or lose it." Garth and family may well have been lost to the ministry of the church because useful ministry was not encouraged.

Diane is one whose story does not smack of superficiality. Her needs were appropriate, yet too well hidden. The church simply failed to meet them. Her cries for help were beyond the listening ear of the untrained caregivers of that congregation.

Diane had left the church several years before our first interview. She had been to Harmony church once during my time in ministry and still considered it the "church I used to go to". Thus she had listed it as her church affiliation during a hospital stay and recognized me when I entered her room. On that first encounter, I met a middle aged woman in full depression over some intense family problems. Having no supportive network in community nor church and an inadequate one in her marriage, she had crumbled under the burden of the delinquent acting out of a teenage child.

A few weeks after Diane returned home I visited her. We had developed a fairly open relationship during her month in hospital and she soon began to talk about the "why" of her present non- affiliation with Harmony Church. I recalled for her the fact that she said she used to go to church regularly, but always alone, and now was never there. "It's such a big church. I'm thinking about going to a little church down the first side road toward Bowmanville." I wondered why she would pick a church that was farther from her home, when she still had friends at Harmony. "I want to go to a smaller church where I can get to know people. When I go to your church it's so big and massive and it doesn't seem all that friendly. We grew up in two small country churches up north and they were so different from going to Harmony."

As we continued our conversation, I pursued the issue of her former life in the Harmony congregation. I wondered aloud about its earlier meanings for her. She admitted, with some apology, that she had never been deeply involved. She used to slip in the back door, take her seat towards the back of the sanctuary, take time for quiet reflection — she said she always liked the organ prelude because it allowed her to think about her life in God's perspective -and then take part in the worship. Music seemed to hold the deepest meaning in the worship for her. When it was over she would slip out quickly, usually with a brief "hello" to the preacher, and then on home alone. She was a loner. That was the way she wanted it. She never stayed for the coffee hour afterward. And she really thought it was awful the way people had gotten to "all this talking before church when they should be alone with God and their thoughts."

Diane is one of those people for whom the congregation's Christian warmth never took! She would call Harmony congregation a cold church. Our later conversations indicated a woman with deep needs which the structure of suburban society was not likely to meet. She felt alone in life. She saw people in a utilitarian way. She experienced the church as a consumer. It was to be called upon at the appropriate needful times in one's journey through life. Yet, one caught the glimpse of the nostalgic country girl who wished more from life. For all her shy standoffish nature, she coveted deep human relationships. But she was not aware how she might turn coveted feelings into the reality of human — even Christian — warmth. And indeed Harmony church had not been helpful in her search toward that end. Very few medium-to-large congregations seem able to help with this all-too-human dilemma.

A brief pastoral footnote: In my clinics I am often asked what the ideal size of a congregation is. The question is usually couched in stories like Diane's. Or, "I don't find my congregation, or any other for that matter, to be very friendly."

My answer is always the same. The ideal size should be 12. I firmly believe that Jesus was correct when he chose "12 to be with him". Yes, he dealt with the massive crowds. Yes, he dealt intensely with individuals in need. But there were only 12 who benefitted from the deep nurturing insights of the day to day struggle of becoming Christian. What Jesus knew, and we so easily forget, is that we can be truly present to only a handful of others at any given point in our human/Christian journey. Congregations which know and live this principle have learned to maximize the church within the congregation concept. The total pastoral life is a composite of smaller clusters within that larger body of believers. They are able to put to theological advantage the small group principle that Jesus used so long ago.

I have always had particular love of our cathedral-like churches. Why? Because in that majestic symbol of our religious heritage, there are no illusions about the warmth of human fellowship. You build it yourself in the human community of persons sitting below the majestic spires. It is a place where paupers and kings may well sit in the same pew... and often where all sit as strangers to each other. People come to that church from all walks of life and usually will not bump into each other again for the next seven days. Yet, spend some time after worship watching what happens. Very few go to the coffee hour. There's not much of a Christian education program either. But... watch the clutches of significant others gather in the narthex, on the lawns, in the parking lot. In their threes and sixes and twelves, they linger for conversation and hugs. Often they go off to a restaurant together to finish this human encounter. And that's what communion is about.

Large churches don't have to be cold. Diane could have found Christian warmth under Harmony's high vaulted ceiling. The congregation must be intentional about it, however, if it is to happen for more than a select few.

There was also a significant surprise in the stories of some others who fall under the general category of those who left because the church did not meet their personal needs. They represent a fairly substantial number of cases. Subsequent conversations with many other dropouts indicate that this may necessitate some fine tuning in the way we balance the pastoral caring and prophetic modes of our ministry.

Let me preface the next story with a brief comment. The agendas of stewardship and evangelization may well be on a collision course in this area. So often we have been told by stewardship experts that if the pulpit deals with some of the controversial issues of our time we will empty the pews. And there is ample evidence that controversial issues dealt with publicly do shift some people from the inside to the outside of the church. Or, at least, shift them between congregations or denominations. However, there is also ample (and increasing) evidence that if the pulpit does not deal with the pressing issues of our time people will also leave.

Like Lanny. A university trained engineer in a middle-management position with General Motors, Lanny felt both powerless and empowered. He had grown up in a union family and knew first hand the advantages of having the collective security of the U.A.W. behind his father on some major issues with that monolith corporate giant of the Motor City. His wider experience in middle management also taught him that labour sometimes sat down on the job and didn't return fair value.

His was a job with considerable responsibility for hiring and firing. He wasn't always comfortable with the choices he had to make, such as the case of one slacker. "Clearly this guy should have been dismissed. He was a detriment to the company. However, he had three years to go before he could get early pension. He used to be a good employee but now something had embittered him. He'd worked for my department for 11 years. His supervisor was on my case to get him out. Medical grounds? Any grounds. Just get rid of him. But I knew a bit more of the story. His wife was unable to work. She'd been disabled for years. They also had two children left at home."

He struggled through that moral dilemma of decision-maker and caring person. In the end, however, he didn't get to make the final decision. The system did. He didn't like the way it was handled, but he was powerless before those who also commanded his destiny.

To make things worse, he felt as if he did — or ought to — have more power in the unfolding drama of life. The ought to came from the Gospel he heard in his church every week. It felt heavy at times. There was always this push to be and do more in society.

And then it happened. You have to live in a one-industry town for only a short while to understand that all the bread and butter — as well as personal — issues come home to roost when you see strike looming large on next month's calendar.

Lanny was distressed. The issues were not all clear. There were points to be made for both the U.A.W. and General Motors. He was upset about the way things were drifting. In his distress he thought it might be good to bounce some of his ideas off his pastor. "Sure as hell couldn't do it with folks at the office, or buddies who work out there on the line."

So they talked. He cried a bit. He swore a bit. He wondered aloud about some of his colleagues. He had some pejoratives about the U.A.W. leadership too. And then he made a suggestion to his pastor. "This is an interesting congregation, Jim, in that it's a pretty good balance of labour and management. What would you think about dealing with the issue of the strike from the pulpit. I would think there is lots of stuff in those prophets you talk about that might be relevant."

The pastor nearly choked. He started to back pedal. He pleaded how close he was to people on both sides. He was afraid of what it might do to some particular people. They might even leave the church. Lanny interrupted. He talked about how he felt "pushed" by what Pastor Jim often said from the pulpit. It made him feel as if the Gospel were meant to be in the world, lived out there. And this was an opportunity to make it specific.

But Pastor Jim kept on back pedalling. Yes, the Gospel was meant to be about our lived experience. But this was different. It was too close. He cared too much about how his people might feel about the issue. He didn't want to hurt any of them. And he never did hurt any of them — by what he said. In the ensuing weeks he said nothing about the strike. Nothing!

Lanny thought late into the night about that conversation. He thought he had put his case well. "And, dammit, the Gospel ought to be about real life. And this strike stuff was as real as life got in Oshawa." Come to think of it, though, he had never heard any real specifics of the Gospel pushing up against the hard realities of life. It had always been generalities. When a real issue arose, the ought of the Gospel fizzled into irrelevancies.

What Lanny needed to hear was not the why of the Gospel but its how and what. He longed to hear a clear "word of the Lord" in his present day experience. And the church had denied it to him. He is like so many others whose stories I have since listened to. They expect the Gospel to have some clear word for the ordinary bread and butter issues of life. They want to know that the Gospel has something to do with where the rubber hits the road on their street. They long for a modern Isaiah and Jeremiah. They want a modern Moses who shows some leadership skills. They want to wait with a Mary or Elizabeth for the unfolding drama of God's becoming in their midst. But what they get is a gutless pulpit.

People want to hear a poignant word of the Lord in our time, and on our time. They want to hear a "thus saith the Lord" about Ronald Reagan and Nicaragua. They want a biblical assessment of Mikhail Gorbachev and his peace proposals. They know God has to do with apartheid and pornography and abortion and child abuse and marriage and divorce. They wanted a word about Vietnam.

And, yes, some people will leave the church. The Gospel will pinch some lives, if spoken truthfully. It will release the yoke and burdens of others. And people will also leave the church if they don't hear the prophetic word of the Gospel. We have to choose which side of the cutting edge of faithfulness we shall be on. A prophetic ministry can indeed be exercised if based on pastoral caring for persons.

But Lanny left the church. He said his integrity demanded it. Like many others, he saw the church as innocuous. Unfortunately he began to see the Gospel too as irrelevant to where life needs to be lived.

C. Changes in Life Style

Significant changes in one or more of the primary factors of a person's life patterns also had a prominent effect on their church affiliation. In my original interview sample, some 36 percent left the church because of what might be termed a change in their life style or life pattern. My continued observation of the dropout tracks of others give me a sense that this figure might even be higher in the general populace.

Affiliation to the life of the church would appear to be dependent upon the continuous development of a person's traditional values, involvements, and state of being. This should not surprise us. Systems analysis has long told us that if you change one significant part of a system, the whole system will be affected. Our lives, indeed, are an intricate maze. When one part of our being changes or develops, then we become new beings with new agendas, taking new paths. In this sense, therefore, when we note significant changes in the lives of people in our congregations, we can readily predict their patterns of affiliation or non-affiliation. How to cope with these is one of the challenging pastoral opportunities of our time.

It is one of the strange facts of Canadian ecclesiastical life that — in most places — the church year does not run the full calendar year. At Harmony church, in the regular church year, between October and May, attendance would be somewhere around 350. But as soon as the 24th of May arrived, with all its recreational invitations, the congregation would slump to about 30. Immediately after the October Thanksgiving weekend, it would pop back up to 350. On first encounter a new pastor might become a little paranoid about her/his preaching and read some personal message into the contemporary exodus of the people of God. Yet s/he could see that there was much sense in what was happening. And hope loomed just beyond the horizon as to corrective measures that might be taken.

Let's share a bit of the journey of Wayne and Lonna. They were a typical young couple in that community. Married ten years, they had two children, a huge mortgage, and a life-long family identity with the east end of the city. Their parents had been founding members of the congregation.

Wayne worked hard as a shop foreman. He made a good wage. It was not quite enough for their economic ambitions. They had a wine taste, but a beer income! So Lonna took a part time job for a couple of years. That made things balance financially, just. Then Lonna got to like the job, and she liked the things it added to their life style. They were able to take a winter cruise every couple of years. The family could go to Florida for the March break. And after all that did do a lot for family life.

Then in April one year, as they tell the story, an opportunity came their way that they could ill afford to miss. A cottage near that of close friends came up for sale. Their friends encouraged them to buy. It was within what they could afford. It would also give them some different family opportunities. So they took possession of their first family cottage in late June.

During May and early June they were in church as usual, almost every Sunday — not like the other 320 or so who had already left for their country estates. They mentioned their new purchase to the pastor and joked that they might not see him so often when the summer breezes blew. He laughed. But he didn't see much more of them — ever!

Harmony was following the track that much of a newly secularized North America was also following. Wayne closed up the cottage in late October that first summer. He had loved the summer there. It had been a special family time, he thought. Over the winter he began to dream a bit, about snowmobiles and cross country skiing. He even had some of those dreams in the midst of the odd Sunday sermon. That next summer he worked late into the nights winterizing their new-found gem of family togetherness.

He had said good-bye to the pastor as they headed north for the second summer. Trouble was, he didn't say hello again that fall or winter. He was gone for the next few years.

He was gone until an occasion put him alongside the recently arrived pastor at a wedding reception. Apologies were profuse. "I mean, you need this time with your family. And it's real tough all year as a shop foreman. Where else can you get that kind of rejuvenation that you need to keep your head above water in these tough times." He did make some points with the new pastor. As a matter of fact, he made just one too many. I was impressed with Wayne. As he told his story of life in the used-to-be church, I was deeply disturbed that we had lost this person from the active ministry of our congregation. I wondered how many more were out there like him. And he got me to dreaming and talking to others like him.

So one night before the next summer exodus I went back and talked to Wayne and Lonna. "I need your help. I want some of your ideas about people who have left. Is there anything we can do to keep them involved, recognizing what you say about the positive nature of cottaging?" There were a few embarrassed comments about "haven't a clue". Then later some ideas started to percolate.

That summer we began to host a city-wide summer service on Thursday evenings. It had a children's program on a minimal basis. Most of the service was intentionally intergenerational. It worked all right but nothing exciting. The problem was that Wayne and Lonna came, a few of their like-minded friends, and then a good many people who were also there on Sunday. They heard the same sermon twice over. (Some of them needed it.)

That winter Wayne and I talked a bit further about it. He said, "Unless you cancel Sunday and put the whole ball of wax on Thursday, it won't work. People still think the real thing only happens on Sunday and what we do in mid-week is just Mickey Mouse." I thought a lot about his comments that winter. I asked, "What's to lose? The 30 come both Thursday and Sunday anyway." So we talked about it in the Official Board. Thankfully Harmony was blessed with creative minds, and part of their creativity was their risking.

That summer we "cancelled Sunday". We told people we were "going fishing". But on Thursday night we celebrated the Lord's Day. We got the full choir out, not just one unemployed soloist who had nothing better to do. We had a full scale Christian education program for all our youth. There were a lot of special features that we found we were able to do. And the pastor went camping weekends with the rest of the folk. Some good things happened because he was in that holiday area with his people that might otherwise not have happened.

Well... that's a bit of stretching the truth. It almost happened, but not quite. But I still dream of a congregation which will dare to take that risk because it believes that the people who have left the church are more important than those of us who have remained. That's a primary principle of missiology and evangelization to which I hold. I don't think the church is here for herself, but for those outside. And I am convinced that the church which takes this kind of suggested radical surgery is not far from the kingdom of God.

Other changes in life style are not so consciously chosen. They are rather given, or inflicted, by the exigencies of life. Like Dora's story.

Her husband, Don, who had been otherwise healthy, died suddenly of a massive heart attack. "I couldn't believe it. He had been so healthy. And what do I do now? Our lives had been so intertwined. We did everything together. I found church real tough to handle. The kids had their own families now. They didn't go to church that often, though. So there I was alone in church, for the first time since I can remember. Let me tell you, it wasn't easy. You preachers have your back to what we lay people face... that cross up there in the front. And if there's anything which reminds you of death, it's that. I had to face that every time I went there. I had never thought about it that way before. But when things change in your life, it changes the way you look at some things too."

Dora's story is typical. A person is used to being in church in a certain togetherness. That bond is no longer there, Don has gone, and she finds church a lonely and difficult place of memory. Many widows find it tough, too tough, and they have to leave. As Dora did.

Another dream. This time a dream which does exist in Harmony. A widows' row! Remember the earlier comments about the "congregation within the church". The widows' row is one such small group, which can become a caring ministry for the newly bereaved. They know much about the wounded healer ministry we shall comment on later. Often they are the best prepared to keep the Doras in the church. They might even help Dora understand how she can be in ministry down the road to another of God's lonely widows or widowers.

Stories of the recently separated and divorced follow much the same pattern as Dora's, but for a slightly different reason. Nor are they the same as the situation of Lyla, who met with inadequate ministry in her time of crisis. Divorce is a difficult event of the human journey. If you have been through it, you know the pain and the guilt and the deep self-questioning. Who am I? How could I have failed so? What an awful person I must be! It wouldn't have happened to me if I were a better person, a better Christian. What does God think of me?

Low self-image spawns readily in the recently divorced person. And church is one of the tough places to be when you are down on yourself. When some uncaring — and out of antiquity — pastor intones, "We most miserable sinners," you know whom s/he is talking to. Hence many of the church dropouts in my research have been among the recently divorced.

As you will have already guessed, the same principle of the church within the congregation needs to be at work here. Christian divorcees/separateds groups are beginning to appear in some of the larger Canadian centres. And since there are many in this situation out there (in our mission zone, we shall later call it), it might be time for some creative imaging on how to use them in the ministry of the kingdom. It is only the wounded who really know how to heal!

Another type of charge among the dropout population is also beginning to become more prominent. My Australian experience indicated this to be an even more significant factor in Australasia. Going up and down the vocational ladder is accounting for a significant number of persons who move out of the church.

Like Wade. In many ways he was one of the more interesting persons I encountered in my early research days. He was a man I intensely admired. He had grown up in the depression. His father had a menial job removing the garbage at one of the plants at "the Motors". "Dad was a good man, a good family man. He tried to give our seven kids all he could offer us. He himself had very little education. That made him feel that it was important for the kids. But it couldn't be much. Not college, and that sort of stuff. When he died I was 17 and that meant as one of the older boys I had to go out to work. Mom needed the support."

Wade's first job, in those tough times, was similar to his father's. He literally began at a similar plant pushing the broom. "But I hung in there. I was a company man, and proud of it. And it has got me well ahead. You can see by my home and the cars in the driveway that I'm not pushing that broom any longer."

Wade became a manager of the market research department at the age of 52. He had been a faithful employee for 34 years by that time. The struggle hadn't been easy. He was intuitive, in terms of the motor industry, but he had also done a lot of work on his own. He was a voracious reader. Few knew the detail he did about the product and how to get it across to the consumer. He also had taken every opportunity available for courses the company offered. Yes, he was "a company man. And proud of it."

But he was also his own man. He meant by that, "I am proud of where I am. I'm the one who has got me where I am." There was data to back him up. He had made it up through tough times. Sheer effort and good Protestant work ethic instilled by his father had got him to the top of the pile.

The trouble was, in a theological sense, that he saw no place for God in the success he had attained. "I did this by myself. What's God got to do with all this?"

Wade has been very active in Harmony church in his more humble days. "It's a stage I have grown out of, I guess. I don't need it any more. Come to think of it, I don't know why I needed it back then either." As he climbed the vocational ladder, his church affiliation began to loosen more and more. He now came for state occasions and for the ever-enjoyable annual turkey dinner.

People who go up the vocational ladder sometimes hold tightly to the belief that I did it all by myself. They jettison God as an archaic encumbrance whom they no longer need in these loftier heights of achievement. On the other hand, those who slide down the vocational ladder suffer from a different malaise. Theirs is a gripping sense of failure and self-deprecation. Many of the middle managers who in the early 1980s found themselves in instant unemployment had self-worth problems of an immense magnitude. More and more, I am talking with church dropouts who have come through that experience and ask, "Where was God when I needed him?" This God-in-the-gaps theology is tough to answer when people know they will never ever have a job close to the former one.

D. Conflict with the Pastor or a Church Member

I had expected, as I indicated earlier, that conflict might be one of the major precipitating factors when persons drop out of the church. However, this did not prove to be the case. In the original research sample only a mere eight percent left because of conflict in their church. Mostly, these were with other church members. Interestingly enough, only one was with the pastor. One would not want to generalize that observation any further. We all know pastors do exist who wander around creating havoc for all who get in their path, and like Samson with the ass's jawbone "wreak disaster everywhere". But so do some prize lay folk also!

We need to face the fact that conflict often does exist in the church. We need also to admit that conflict should exist in the church! Creative conflict is one of those gifts God gives for the growth of the Body. We do mature and become more than we are when faced with the struggles and problems (which we ought better to call opportunities) of the human dilemma. Creative conflict must exist in the church for the sake of its maturity. On the other hand, there often is what might be called destructive (or pathological) conflict. Of such there ought to be none in that church patterning itself after the kingdom of God. But alas there often is in churches which by reason of being in the human community express their nature in all too human ways.

One of my tragic observations in working with clergy around the dropout problem is that all too often they assume an inordinate amount of blame for the dropouts from their church. They assume that because Mr. and Ms. Smith have become disaffiliated, they — the clergy — are the cause. They are paying themselves far too high a compliment. Much research indicates that clergy are the cause in only a small percentage of cases. Nonetheless, when they note that Mr. Smith has gone, and Mrs. Jones no longer comes, they blame themselves.

As a result, pastors work overtime at their defense mechanisms. Because it is their fault, they are the last ones to go to see Smith and Jones. Also because it is their fault, they don't ask anyone else to go either. A visitor might discover what a failure the pastor has been. Thus the church dropouts are left alone to their pain and turmoil (no matter what the reason for their leaving might have been).

The exact opposite pastoral behaviour is called for. Since pastors are generally not the reason people leave, they may well be the means to bring them back. Generally they are the best trained in pastoral caring and hence, uniquely gifted to help. If perchance they were the cause, then they had better screw up courage and take what's coming.

E. A Crisis of Faith

A significant percentage of people in the original research sample — almost 10 percent — dropped out of church life because of what one might call a crisis of faith. As indicated earlier, these are persons whose faith and present life circumstances are not congruent. What they believe does not match with what they do.

My continuing conversations with church dropouts would indicate that this percentage is now considerably higher. As life has become more complex, in terms of vocational as well as personal issues, the emotional and spiritual conflicts that people find themselves in are much more numerous. This is true for the demands placed on them in their vocation, decisions that have to be faced in personal life, as well as just what the deck of life seems to deal out to us.

Predictably we are often in the area of conflicting claims of good and evil. We feel a bit like the ancient Job when trying to understand what life is up to about us. The answer is beyond our real understanding. Ask Marlene.

Marlene was one of the more delightful persons I met in the original research population. She told the story of her father's horrendous death. She was, at that time, a faithful Christian and watched this parent die, inch by inch. This parent also was a believing Christian who talked on his deathbed about a "loving father God". With as much conviction as she could muster she told me, "and that's such a crock of... " The faith fibre of her life rotted away when she could not hold together the concepts of a "loving father God" and a God who would not help her dying father. The problem of sin and evil will always smash itself on the anvil of human faithfulness. Some will be broken by it. Others will merely leave the church as a way of speaking out against God and the community of faith.

I remember our first meeting as if it were yesterday. I knocked on her front door wearing a clerical collar (thank God). The door opened a few inches, held at that minimal opening by a chain lock. She peered out skeptically as I introduced myself, indicating why I was there. "I'm wanting to talk with people who used to be part of the life of Harmony church and now don't come. I'd like to hear something of their story."

Marlene indicated that she had not let anyone in the house for the past five years. "You can come in for a couple of minutes... but just for a couple of minutes." So I took whatever she was willing to permit and sat down where she indicated. I soon discovered that the chained door was a necessity for a

woman who was warding off the outside world totally. She had
lived only to herself and her husband for several years, with
the rare exception of a trip to her psychiatrist. Her tattered
housecoat and pin curlers in mid-afternoon completed the stereotypical picture of the neurotically depressed woman totally
overcome by life.

The first few minutes of our conversation were hesitant
ones. She said very little. There was little to which I could
respond. So after about ten minutes I rose to leave. But she
stopped me. Somewhat hesitantly she suggested that I might
stay longer and have a cup of tea with her. "I haven't talked
with anyone for so long I'd like to talk about some things in
the church a bit." So I stayed for 20 minutes, an hour, and then
it turned into an hour and a half. Our visit was only interrupted
by a returning and absolutely shocked husband. He had not
known her to have any visitors for some time. It took a little
while for Marlene to realize she could say what she thought.
Then Marlene turned to some of the reasons she left the church.
She talked with deep emotion — almost a present tense emotion — of her father who had died some seven years before.
"My dad and I were very close. He was the best friend I've
ever had." I noted that that was a high compliment to pay to
one's father and invited her to share more about her parent.
She did so willingly. The catalogue of his health afflictions,
according to her telling, would nominate him for candidacy in
a modern play on the biblical Job. And it was here that the
issue of good and evil was rubbed raw for Marlene.

She described in vivid colour her memories of his
lengthy hospitalization with his terminal disease. Long hours
were spent at his bedside, accompanied by many tears for this
father who was "her best friend". A lot of time to reflect, while
he succumbed to a drugged sleep, on who was God and why
could God allow this to happen. She came up with few credible
answers.

"He was such a good man. It didn't seem reasonable
that he should have this kind of life. Always, as long as I can
remember, he had problems and trouble and yet, you know
what almost his last words were before he died? 'Be steadfast
in the faith.'"

Those words had understandably etched themselves in

Marlene's memory. They haunted her for the next years that she stayed in the life of Harmony church and became a key factor marking her exodus. "He talked to me that last night about a loving father God. There he was, with all that pain and suffering, knowing he would soon die, and he talked like that. Almost like his last will and testament. That night he died. I wanted to curse God and die also. Do you know what that's like?" I nodded that I did (and that became one of the solid building blocks from which we later moved to a mutually caring and evangelical relationship).

She ended that part of our conversation pointedly. "What he said was such a crock of... " As she went on to talk about leaving the church some months later, she claimed this life experience as her reason. "I just didn't have any faith left any more. It all seemed to disappear. I guess it shouldn't. I suppose one should believe even in adversity, but I'm not able to, and now it all seems like so much nonsense. She concluded that it was difficult to believe that a good God can let people suffer as her father had.

I spent many afternoons and evenings in Marlene's company after that initial interview. Her own life had also been one of illness and turmoil. Most of it was psychiatric, compounded by this experience with her father. Not much of her life would have given her reason to believe, given the fact that she chose to believe that because God is in heaven all should be right with the world. It seemed as if the book of Job had escaped her critical biblical eye.

Marlene continues to this day a good friend. She is one who has helped me with my own journey. I continue to care for her deeply, and she for me. She has never quite managed to return to the church. But she does practice her faith regularly and intentionally. To her story we shall return in a later chapter.

OTHER POSSIBILITIES

Regrettably, there has been very little research on the church dropout. Church bureaucrats and programmers had some assumptions about why these persons left the faith community. There has been, however, very little hard data. Even now most of the hypotheses put forward are guesses. They are not based on empirical research, captured in conversation with those who have left us.

The first person to do major research with the stories of the dropouts was John Savage, now president of LEAD Consultants. Savage is a Methodist pastor, formerly noted for his work in education. In the process of doing research for the Doctor of Ministry degree at Colgate Rochester/Bexley Hall/Crozer Theological Seminaries, in 1973-74, he trained a number of Methodist clergy to interview 101 persons in four upstate New York Methodist congregations.

The interviewees were selected according to three categories of church involvement: those who were very active, less active, and inactive. Savage wanted to develop a scheme for understanding the signals people gave and the emotional/spiritual processes of detachment that people developed as they moved further away from the centre of the church. He later hoped to develop some training modules to help clergy and lay persons minister more effectively to those moving down what he calls "the church dropout track". Some readers will be aware of Savage's Lab I and Lab II programs, which are the modules developed after his research. They are excellent training opportunities for persons taking seriously the pain of church dropouts and wanting to be helpful to those outside the life of the institutional church.

The basic premise of Savage's research was that people begin to move onto the church dropout track after some precipitating, anxiety-provoking event. The subsequent anger results in an attitude of either boredom or apathy towards the church. Some years later, Savage indicated to me that it is more appropriate to talk of a cluster of events rather than a single event. In a very helpful way, he also indicates that the stages one moves through to become a hardcore dropout can be identified. The first cries for help can be heard, if the caregivers have the ears to hear. Only later is the exodus evident through such things as changes in church attendance or related activities.

I believe that Savage's contribution to the literature on church dropouts, (3) is among the most helpful available. It needs some cultural redefinition for Canadians, like all Americana, but comes closer than any parallel Canadian attempts at understanding. His training events merit serious consideration by Canadian Christian leaders.

American Roman Catholics have also recently become fascinated with their church dropout population. Alvin Illig of the Catholic Bishops' Centre for Evangelization in Washington, D.C., has become a listening post for a number of persons who have left the Roman Catholic church. His newsletters, over the past couple of years, indicate that there are probably six main reasons for Catholic dropouts. Primary among these are family problems, such as divorce. Second, the competing value system of a materialistic life style has caused a deterioration of family life on which Catholicism depends. A third reason is the poor preaching evident in many Catholic parishes and the lack of emphasis on spiritual growth. Paralleling this is the fact that many people feel that worship services are poorly prepared and conducted. For people exposed to sophisticated media, the church appears mediocre in its public presentations. Dull and uninteresting, they say! Conflict with the pastoral staff comes a distant fifth in his explanation of dropout patterns. This is an interesting parallel to our Canadian learnings. Finally, there is a feeling among these dropouts that it doesn't matter if they are there. They indicate that they would not be missed if they stayed away. Hence, the issue of finding meaningful involvement in faith life, what we would call ministry or discipleship, also exists for the Roman Catholic dropout population. It seems that "use them or lose them" is a fundamental principle to keeping members in the church.

In a straightforward and helpful book titled simply *The Unchurched (Who They Are And Why They Stay Away)* Russell Hale categorized 10 types off people who are outside the church. This distinguished white-haired, winsome and soon-to-retire professor of church and community at Lutheran Theological Seminary in Gettysburg, Pennsylvania, took a year's sabbatical leave from teaching and wandered through the most disparate counties of America interviewing people on the streets, in restaurants or in their homes. He chose those counties which statistically had the lowest figures for church involvement. His book is full of stories, as the author is himself a marvellous teller of human stories.

The first category is the anti-institutionalists. These people say they are on the outside (and not necessarily looking in) because they experience the church as being preoccupied with maintaining its own self. They see our organizational structures as diametrically opposed to what they believe religion should be, and they object strongly to in-church politics. Our ministries, they note, are irrelevant to the real needs of humanity.

A second group of persons called themselves the boxed in. Their former lives in the church left them feeling restrained or controlled. Some felt constrained by doctrine or ethics which were too narrow for their current life experience. Others felt thwarted by the church. Instead of finding affiliation a nurturing experience, they found that it held back their movement toward maturity. They felt the church treated them like children or, at best, adolescents. Some even viewed the church as similiar to living in a prison. They experienced it as something which limited freedom rather than set them free.

One might have expected to find his third category. They were the burned out. They felt that the church had depleted their resources, talents and time. In their church life they had become overly involved and (in most cases) when they moved to another community they were glad to be rid of the continual demands of their former church life.

The floaters, if they had ever been part of the church, had been only on the periphery. They never did put down roots. They were infrequent in attendance and involvement. Essentially they never did have any deep feelings about what the church did or said. Perhaps they just never wanted the responsibility that goes with believing. It was easier to stay out on the edge.

The hedonists are ones who find life's meaning in the pursuit of pleasure and happiness. All of life's journey is aimed at self- fulfillment. To be involved in church-related activities would be counter productive. Faith doesn't always, or usually, give instant gratification. You have to wait for the fullness of the kingdom, even while living in it. Understandably, many of these people were located in the sunbelt states such as California and Florida. Some of their not-too- distant cousins probably have addresses in Victoria and Vancouver and Toronto.

Then there were the locked out. They had experienced the strong arm of the gate keepers who didn't give them permission to become meaningfully involved in the life of the church. Some of these heartless permission givers act as if they own the church when they have merely been called into stewardship of the Body of Christ. They close doors against people, rather than open them, and sow seeds of disillusionment rather than grains of faith. Hence, some outsiders in Hale's research indicated they felt rejected, some neglected, and others blatantly discriminated against.

A seventh category he called the nomads. These are wanderers, rovers with no fixed address. Vocation has transferred them from place to place. Community is always temporary. As for emotional investment in friends, forget it! Fellowship is something they cannot define.

Pilgrims were an interesting category. We in the church often use that word to describe ourselves. Pilgrims felt their religious views were still in the process of formation. They wanted to look at all the options before they could say "yes" to any. The chief mark of this group was their tentativeness.

There were also the publicans, who made up the largest group of Hale's interviewees. They talked of the church people they knew as hypocrites, phonies, people living double lives, or fakers. From their vantage point, on the outside looking in, they noted the difference between our profession and performance. For themselves they claim a convenient agnosticism, because they would be unable to live up to the expectations the faith holds out to the faithful.

And finally, the true unbelievers. Hale found few authentic unbelievers. That is not surprising, if George Gallup is right that over 95 percent of Americans believe in God. But some did insist that that utimate Reality is unknown or unknowable.

While Hale's research did not specifically deal with people who were once inside and now were outside, there is much in his typology that commends itself to us in our consideration of the church dropout. The dropout is not the same as the unchurched in type, need or ministry agenda. Many have never experienced church life, or their former involvement was so minimal as to be just an inoculation against a real faith. We have to keep in mind that Hale's analysis, however helpful, covers a much broader spectrum than our concern in this book.

One significant piece of research has just been completed in Canada. Reginald Bibby undertook a mammoth sampling of opinion of both active and inactive Anglicans in the Diocese of Toronto. The study, released in April of 1986, was appropriately called Anglitrends. (4) Since I was involved in the project's early planning stages, I have kept close tabs on the Bibby findings. I have also reflected on the implications of Bibby's research for other Canadian faith communities, such as the United Church.

The research was not directed specifically toward understanding the church dropout. Rather, it wanted to understand how the opinions of activeand inactive Anglicans differed on a wide range of issues. However, Bibby's research does indicate a major reason and some minor reasons why the inactives became inactive. Their lessened activity was primarily due to "preferred use of time elsewhere". In my own research sample, 72 percent left the church because of a change in life style or because the church was not meeting their personal needs.

In Bibby's study, some minor reasons given for church withdrawal were changes in the worship services, a shift in their own goals, and a perceived excessive emphasis upon money by the church. Since the liturgy is so central to Anglicanism, one might expect this to be more of a factor for their church's dropouts. My own sense is that among Reformed churches the shifts in liturgy have had a minimal effect. We are more likely to lose people if the preaching is not up to snuff. (It is strange, too, that poor preaching was indicated as a cause of dropouts among the Roman Catholics in America, another liturgically-centred church.) Bibby's research is primarily focused on the recent emphasis on social issues and justice-oriented concerns by the Anglican hierarchy. But he found the laity more concerned with personal moral and ethical issues than with corporate or systemic moral issues. Regrettably, where the parish priest or the Primate have focused on these wider issues, they have been received generally with a yawn. (This might well be the case for many Reformed congregations too.) Again this reflects what some of my Harmony friends said about the church not meeting their personal needs.

The main thrust of Anglitrends is on what Toronto Anglicans want from their church. For those who are active, the primary issue centres around compartmentalization. They allow the church to influence only very specialized parts of their lives. It no longer is their social centre. Other activities and interests often predominate.

The inactive Anglicans (perhaps you might want to think in terms of dropout Anglicans here) use the church, when they do, for a slightly different reason. Bibby uses the term "consumption without commitment". The inactives come to the church for those rites of passage that are necessary in our culture. Weddings, baptisms and funerals. They also come for counsel when they are at wit's end, and wonder if God might have a wit to give to their human dilemma. I suspect this pattern will become an increasing one, and not only for Anglicans. We are all like reasonably well-fed people coming to the banquet table of life, on which are spread all the goodies of our world. Religion and faith are but a few of the delicacies available. We take from that banquet table only the goodies which meet our fancy, or our need. This means that the church is in a highly competitive marketplace. If we are to survive we need to be deeply aware of what it is we are offering . And we must offer it well and with credibility.

CHAPTER VII
THE UNCHURCHED AMERICAN:
WISDOM ON THE GALLUP

Oftimes church leaders look disparagingly at the latest research issued by The Gallup Organization. We seem to be suggesting that their sampling of popular opinion need not be taken seriously. I would suggest that this opinion places much of our work in missiology in jeopardy. We can ill afford to ignore wisdom on the Gallup!

In 1978 the Gallup Organization teamed with the Princeton Religion Research Centre to undertake a study for The Religious Coalition of backgrounds, values and interest of the unchurched Americans. Thirty-one religious groups and denominations had become conscious that some 61 million American adults were not members of any church or religious institution. They wanted to know what makes them tick and how they might become more meaningfully engaged in ministry to them. It was a mammoth research undertaking which involved interviewing 3,062 persons in the two categories of the unchurched and the churched.

How did the study define the unchurched? Their definition included "any person who is not a member of a church or synagogue or who has not attended a church or synagogue in the last six months, apart from weddings, funerals, or special holidays such as Christmas, Easter, or Yom Kippur." This category is much wider than what we have been referring to as church dropouts. Nonetheless, there is something for us to learn from the survey which is helpful for our faithful responses to ministry with the Canadian church dropout.

The American scene has been little different from the Canadian one in terms of church drainage. Most mainline Protestant denominations have suffered losses of at least 10 percent. Some have lost as many as 25 percent of their membership. The Roman Catholic Church, whose membership statistics are difficult to ascertain, would appear to have suffered even deeper losses than Protestants. (They also have been much better at recovery.)

There has also been a dearth of convincing remedies. Yet eight in 10 Americans continue to say that they believe that Jesus Christ is God or the Son of God. A supposed generation of believers, according to all the Gallup work done in 1952, 1965 and 1978, is giving birth to a nation of non-belongers as far as religious affiliation is concerned. Of those thousands questioned, at least eight in 10 indicated that one can be a good Christian or Jew and not attend church or synagogue.

Some of the hypotheses, before the research was undertaken, were similar to ours in Canada. People are leaving the church because we are moving into a highly secularized time in which religious interest is declining. This is a rootless generation. We move around so easily that one tends not to put down roots in community. (You haven't yet unpacked your bags, and don't intend to because soon you'll move again.) Some also suggested that it is a day of non-institutionalism.

Some of the findings of the *Unchurched American* survey that I believe shed some helpful light on our Canadian situation are as follows:

First, Americans are divorcing their religious beliefs from religious affiliation. Believing and belonging are no longer synonymous. An increasing multitude are not against the church's presence in society; just do not see its relevance to their life.

A second finding is that Americans have changed very little in their spiritual beliefs. Sixty-four percent of the un-churched sample believe that Jesus is divine. Seventy percent indicate that the Bible is divinely inspired. Some 50 percent believe in life after death, and a majority of those outside the church indicate that religion is important to them. Over 75 percent say they pray to God, with 50 percent saying they do so daily. This is not an irreligious generation. Things have not changed that much, with the exception of going to church. People feel no need of such religious institutional involvement.

What is the reason? In part, it can be found in the unchurched's attitude toward the institution called church. On the public confidence scale, the church was further down than it had ever been before. Only 38 percent of the unchurched expressed much confidence in the church as an institution. On the other hand 80 percent of the churched felt a great deal of confidence in the church as an institution. What is the reason for this loss of esteem? It seems mainly due to the belief that the church has lost the real spiritual part of religion. The accusation is that we, the church, have beome too concerned with organizational as opposed to spiritual and theological issues. They also feel that the church is not very effective in helping people find meaning in their lives and not very adept at doing justice in the social realm. It sounds a bit like Canadian church dropouts speaking, doesn't it?

Reginald Bibby warned Canadians a few years ago that we needed to hear the cry for meaning and fill this religious vacuum with the good news of the Gospel. He went so far as to note that the church was in the "meaning business" and if we failed people there, we would fail them essentially, and they would leave the church in droves. His observation is apparently true for Americans as well. They expect to find meaning for their lives in the church, and have not done so. At least, that is what their stories would attest. Might this also be one of the central issues for the unchurched Canadian?

I suspect that the search for meaning is a substantive issue on both sides of the border, perhaps the main issue. It needs to be addressed more intentionally in terms of the church dropout. Lack of meaning is surely central to the issues of inadequate ministry in crisis times. It is true also when one feels the church is not addressing one's perceived personal needs. Perhaps the church can help to rediscover meaning for persons when life's changes happen, either intentionally or unintentionally. Remember Marlene? Her cries for help around the issue of good and evil were surely part of a perceived meaninglessness on her life's journey. I suspect Bibby knows much more about us than we would care to listen to. And Gallup too!

American researchers and evangelization programmers are still at work on the Unchurched American. They haven't fully realized how to deal with her/him. However, they continue to work at it. There is considerable hope for the future because their studies have made both clergy and laity aware of the deep, underlying causes of church drainage. Church leaders need to keep in mind that a quarter of the 91 million churchgoing adults themselves had a period of two or more years when they did not go to church. More important, however, is the fact that 52 percent of the currently unchurched could imagine circumstances under which they would return to church life.

To that task of helping the church dropouts drop back in, we now turn!

PART II:
DROPPING BACK IN

CHAPTER VIII
"ON THE OTHER SIDE OF ME":
MORE THAN A SONG

The car radio was on as I travelled from Oshawa to
Toronto. My mind was on the conversations I had been having
in recent days with those persons who had left Harmony
Church. As I had listened to their stories, it seemed as if deep
was crying unto deep. I couldn't quite put name and form to
it, but these folk were clearly asking for something which the
church, in their experience, had not offered them.

Some of their stories had seemed so superficial. They
were looking for any convenient excuse to be believers but not
belongers. And yet in all their stories was also something very
human. I sensed that most of them really wanted to belong.
And they felt, at deep levels, that they had been forced into
leaving. What was it all about? Like the song said, "what's it
all about, Alfie?" I mused upon that haunting question as my
car sped toward yet another meeting about the mission of the
church. Suddenly I was arrested in my train of thought by a
song on the radio. Something in the lyrics caught my attention.
It set in focus some of the things I had been hearing from those
church dropouts. I called the radio station when I arrived in
Toronto, got the name of the piece and bought it. With record
in hand I later headed home to listen to its lyrics over and over
again.

Small wonder it had caught my attention. Neil Sedaka

put into words the formless pleas that I had been hearing over the past several months. God does move in strange and mysterious ways. Even through car radios.

"You think you know me pretty well,
But how can you tell?
You never get inside my head.
The times we talk,
We never speak,
We play hide and seek.
So many things are left unsaid.

Why can't you see what's on the other side of me?
The side of me that reaches out to you,
Don't let me hide these feelings that have been
    denied.
Only you can set me free.
See what's on the other side of me."

As I listened to that song time and again, I sensed that at last I was dealing with the fundamental question of the church dropout. It was indeed more than a song for me. "Why can't you (that is, we, the caring church) see what's on the other side of me?" — the one who is now on the outside looking in, the church dropout.

It is tough to see and acknowledge what is on the other side of another person. It's tough enough to see and acknowledge what is on the underside of one's own self. We hide so well some sides of ourselves from the world, and even from ourselves. Small wonder that the pain and turmoil of persons moving toward the dropout track remains unnoticed by their colleagues in the local church. And yet it is a side which reaches out to others in strange and sometimes distancing ways. It is a side which can be heard and experienced if we have the eyes to see and ears to hear.

And that brings us to the meaning and practice of pastoral conversation... which is what this book is primarily about. Or almost to it...

One single line of that song lingered with me as I went to bed that night thinking about many of my recent interviews. I couldn't get Marlene out of my mind and several others too.

"Only you can set me free. See what's on the other side of me." Could it be possible that the departure of Marlene and others could have been prevented? Was there a way that I could have heard their cries of helplessness and meaninglessness, if I had been with them? Might it be possible that those cries could be re-heard or re-experienced even now, years later? And if this might be true, could they be helped to understand how to experience "what's on the other side of me" in such a way that the church's drainage could be slowed to a mere trickle? I dared to hope!

And I have lived enough years since then to be part of nudging that hope into reality.

And now that does bring us to the meaning of pastoral conversation.

CHAPTER IX.
PASTORAL CARE VS EVANGELIZATION

Pastors have one task but several functions. Their task is to bring others into a conscious interdependent relationship with Jesus Christ as Lord and Saviour and to nurture them as they learn to live their faith in the real world. And, yes, I did say interdependent. Christ is dependent on us for the exercise of discipleship in the world, just as we are dependent on Christ for the gift and discovery of faith and our subsequent journey.

In ministry, however, there are several functions. For those in professional ministry these include preacher, liturgist, counsellor, pastor, teacher, social activator, and evangelist. The same is largely true for the lay person in a congregation where all ministry is shared. In the life of the church it is necessary that there be an essential unity and compatibility of the many roles so that the integrity of ministry may be whole.

When dealing with the church dropout are we in the area of pastoral caring (the pastor) or in the area of evangelization (the evangelist)? As one reads the history of the church — let alone sees the practice of these two modes of ministry in contemporary life — one notes that they are apparently diametrically opposed. Pastoral care is not evangelism, and evangelism isn't pastoral caring? Or is it? Or can it become that?

Perhaps I should confess at this point to being a confirmed pastoral caregiver. All ministry is — or ought to be — pastoral care. That was the way I was reared in ministry. I see no reason in mature years to change that perception.

The pastoral care function broadly covers four separate

objectives. Seward Hiltner identified the three primary functions of the pastor as healing, sustaining and guiding. To this, George Clebesch and Herbert Jaekle have added a fourth, namely, reconciling. (7) Healing aims at overcoming some impairment by restoring persons to wholeness and leading them to further potential of personhood. Sustaining assists the hurting person to live with or transcend a situation which cannot be altered. Guiding helps the troubled person to choose between alternatives facing them, to the end that their wholeness may be realized. Reconciling seeks to fulfil the Gospel mandate of reconciliation between humanity and God as well as between persons. As pastoral caregivers, we need to keep all four objectives in mind. One of the more useful resources I have found in helping me understand ministry has been one of Hiltner's later books. He wrote *Ferment in the Ministry* in an attempt to give cartoon images as well as theological substance to the work of ministry. (8) In that work he identifies nine images of ministry, among them the image of evangelizing and shepherding (his own particular image for the caring function).

Hiltner portrays the minister as the modern shepherd kneeling beside a sheep with leg caught, Chevrolet in background, first-aid kit spread behind him, and binoculars temporarily laid beside the first-aid kit. His image stresses the solitariness of the attention given to the one sheep, the attention the modern shepherd gives to the concrete need of the captured or wounded lamb, and the use of modern insight and methodology to heal that need.

He also gives a second image which is useful for a more comprehensive understanding of caring. This he calls the clinical image (most appropriate for the father of the modern clinical pastoral education movement). Here the cartoon sees the minister making a bedside call upon a parishioner in hospital. A Bible, or some other symbol of the office of the minister, along with the fact that s/he is seated, illustrate that his/her ministry of caring is exercised through pastoral conversation. It is that because it includes both listening and responding.

So what is the difficulty with pastoral care vs evangelization? Essentially it is the difficulty laid on us by stereotypes. These have dictated that most persons in ministry have seen themselves as one or the other; to be both is schizophrenic.

They have assumed that the basic theological assumptions are diametrically opposed to each other. They have lifted them up, in their extremes, through the exponents of the revivalist tradition under Billy Graham or Oral Roberts on the one hand, or under the caring function with such leading exponents as Seward Hiltner, and Carl Rogers in another camp. As such they have not caught the holism of either. And, hence, pastoral care and evangelism have not been able to be seen as congruent.

The search then is to discover a total understanding of evangelism. I believe the images of Hiltner point to such in the field of pastoral caring. We need an understanding of evangelization which is, on the one hand, not manipulative or seductive nor ruthless in achieving its end of commitment to Christ and the reign of God, but is, on the other hand, directed toward people's growth in faith and owning the faith gains which are appropriate to them at each stage of their personal journey under God.

A biblical evangelization must be concerned with the gospel of personal salvation as well as the gospel of social salvation. Change in an individual's personal relationship to Jesus Christ as the centre of their being is indeed fundamental to their functioning as a whole person. Thus the saving of souls, the creation of new beings in Christ Jesus, is indeed the work of evangelization. But so is the humanization of life through restructuring society and removing every impediment that restricts humanity's fulfilment. Evangelization is thus dealing with that which sins against the possibilities of human existence as much as it is dealing with the sinning of persons in their personal, societal and systemic involvements in life.

A biblical evangelism must be both/and. It cannot be either/or. The life and ministry of Jesus Christ give evidence of the challenge for personal change in terms of repentance and faith in preparation for the coming reign of God. The early church called for the internal change of persons and their commitment to a Person in preparation for the coming kingdom. But both Jesus and the early church also challenged those elements in the social, moral and political worlds which laid strictures on the corporate and individual lives of people. It was a call to repentance and growth for both persons, structures and the world. That was the evangelization of the early church and our Lord.

It is helpful for us to look to the New Testament context of evangelism. The word is not often used. It appears in only three places. Ephesians 4:11 lists the evangelist as one of the ministries along with apostles and prophets. II Timothy 4:5 implies that the work of the evangelist is part of the full ministerial calling. One of the few explicit models, however, is in Acts 8:26-40. In this model we find hopeful possibilities for a happy marriage and continuing life for pastoral care and evangelism.

Philip is directed by divine insight to go to where the field of evangelization is to be. It is one of those God nudges that we so often receive, yet more often than not ignore. Go on the road to Gaza! The subject of evangelizaion is given, the Ethiopian. We often consider him to be a churchperson, but more particularly, he is an enquirer after faith. He is on the outside looking in. He is reading the prophet Isaiah as he travels. But he finds it difficult to understand. He needs an interpreter. The Ethiopian invites the evangelist to join him in his carriage and share with him his journey of faith. And Philip began where the Ethiopian was — not at some previously determined preaching point — and began to share with him a pilgrimage that led ultimately to sharing the Good News of Jesus Christ.

The Ethiopian accepts the challenge, makes the commitment, and enters the fellowship of the church through the waters of baptism. This completes one of the great stories of evangelization in the New Testament witness. That is how evangelization happened in the early church.

Some things ought to be highlighted. Evangelization was on a one to one basis. It was based on the principle of sharing — sharing stories. Most important of all, it began where the interviewee was. His needs, his moment in time, his hidden agenda were all part of the process of that conversation. And it was both pastoral and evangelistic. Philip earned the right to share something, more through his attentiveness to the present struggle of the Ethiopian than by demand or pushiness. The process also went somewhere, for the Ethiopian made a commitment of faith. In evangelistic terms, he had grown toward the objective of faith. However, he had done it on his own schedule, coupled with the nudging of the Spirit of God, and via the nurturing of the one who was also committed to the task of being a channel of God's grace.

I believe these things the biblical witness allows us to claim as learnings for our evangelistic task. And perhaps more.

CHAPTER X
PASTORAL CONVERSATION:
THE MODUS OPERANDI

I have a hunch that the apparent reticence to doing evangelism in mainline denominations is the result of a concept of this particular function of the church. That reticence is coupled with guilt, for devoted mainline Christians feel in their hearts that they ought to be about evangelism but their heads tell them to stay away. I suspect our hang up with this essential of the Christian faith is due to over-kill. Evangelism is what the big name 'televangelists' (whom many of us see as masters of manipulation and theological dishonesty) do. It is not what I — ordinary Jane/Joe Christian — can do or want to do.

We fail to see that this concept of evangelization is indeed limited, and it is limiting to the church and her ministry. Those who do evangelism as revivalism, and do it well and with integrity, indeed do a great service to the building of the kingdom. However, it is not the role or vocation of most of us who call ourselves evangelizers.

Why? The answer is simple. Surprisingly it is an answer that may have been reached by the Billy Graham organization, although I am unable to substantiate this. In any case, it radically altered the way the Graham organization has prepared for its revivals during the past few years.

An article on their research published in The United Church Observer in 1978 startled some evangelists. It indicated that new members came into the church for a number of reasons, but not in the percentages we generally seem to assume. Six to eight percent simply walked in off the street; two to three percent were attracted by some advertised church program; eight to 10 percent came because of the reputation of, or from some contact with the pastor, often in a crisis. Another three to four percent came as a result of the church meeting a specific need in their lives. Only one to two percent responded because of a community visitation program done by the church. Three to four percent came through the Sunday School program (which would likely be different in the USA from Canada because of the adult education focus of many American denominations). Evangelistic preaching resulted in .0005 percent coming into the church. All the rest, some 70 to 80 percent, came into the church because a relative or a friend brought them.

These findings radically changed the focus of the Billy Graham revivalist missions. They began to realize that the preparatory period for their missions was likely more important than the actual mission itself. They had to face the fact, as much mission evangelism does not, that those in attendance at their services were the already converted. Many of those who walked the sawdust trail had blisters on their feet from having walked it before. This was not evangelism; this was evangelical celebration. And indeed there is an essential difference.

Evangelization is what the church does to the world outside herself. It is not what the Body of Christ does to herself, or within its own membership. Important as nurture and celebration are to the church, they are not evangelism.

Hence, the Graham organization turned its focus on getting the already convinced to reach out to their network of friends, acquaintances and colleagues in the work place to suggest their coming with them. It was friend inviting friend, relative suggesting the possibility of meaning for another relative.

The bottom line is that one-to-one evangelization works; crusade evangelism is passe. Or rather the latter is dependent on the former. The face-to-face "being the Christian story" in the various places of life is the essence of what evangelization is about in this latter part of the 20th century.

Hence, we need to identify the importance of pastoral conversation as the *modus operandi* for the evangelizer. It is a recognition that the task of the evangelizer — the one who is being, doing and telling the Christian story — is very ordinary stuff, and for the ordinary persons who call themselves by the name of Christ. And quite frankly those who do it easiest, and best, are those not encumbered by professionalism. Lay persons are the best evangelizers; they are generally the best at pastoral conversation. By reason of vocation they are often more strategically situated in ordinary life and have already built the bridges of God which are essential to the task of evangelization.

Conversation is the essence of human interaction. When we are most truly human we are in conversation, a communion one with the other and with God. We often assume that conversation is about words, yet it is often the unspoken feelings that convey the deepest truths. Our eyes dance, our body gives warmth and acceptance, our smiles indicate we have been understood in a deeper-than-words way. Heije Faber, who first coined the term pastoral conversation, used to say that "it is not the exchange of words but the feelings that determine the shape of our conversations." Conversation has really happened when feelings are truly felt, accepted and acknowledged. Indeed that is when we know that someone sees "what's on the other side of me." In those accepting human moments we sense that we have been freed to become what we might not otherwise be.

Ordinary talk lets us be; pastoral conversation encourages us to become. So the question and searching of those on the outside looking in becomes an all embracing exclamation point. At least, it can become so.

The reader will soon begin to recognize that I am unashamedly Rogerian in my approach to the nature of pastoral conversation. Just to remind us of the Rogerian beginning, from which we shall spring to the consideration of pastoral conversation as the operating frame work for the evangelizer, let me say a word about the five basic tenents from which we begin.

For the psychologist Carl Rogers (and for the writer), human conversation is built upon acceptance, empathetic understanding, significant reflection, clarification and integration.

These are the pillars around which pastoral conversation for evangelism is also built.

Acceptance in conversation means a relationship in which the warmth of personal presence is primary; coercion and pressure are absent. The interchanges permit the maximum of expression, feelings, attitudes and concerns of the one listened to. It is to live in their space for a moment of time and to see that space as sacred and acceptable. It is an affirmation of their right to be who they are!

Normally, and naturally, we hedge our relationships with people by evaluation and conditions. They may be all right, but we are the one who is right and most fully understands. We assess their journey, values and actions by the tried and true mark of our own rightness. Hence we have begun the conversation from a plane above them. True human acceptance, however, will have none of this. Instead it encourages a climate that accepts the person as gifted, as child of God, an equal in every way. There is no devaluing, only valuing. Hence that person is allowed in the conversation to come into the open with the essential person they are and to move toward the possibility of "becoming".

Empathetic understanding, the second tenet, means truly to be beside the other person. Or, perhaps, it means to be inside the other person. It means to sense "the side of me that reaches out to you". More than just feeling for that person, it is to *be* that person as much as is possible. It is to recognize the oneness of the journey you are sharing with them. The ability to feel inside what the other is feeling is the essence of what we mean. It is our native sister's invitation to walk two miles in her moccasins and to speak the word of truth only after we have done that.

Perhaps it is what Lloyd Banyon was saying to me in our fourth conversation. By this time we had shared much of the pain he and his family felt for the loss of young Ron. We had talked and cried together about some parallel pains in our similar journeys. We had been angry at God together — and indeed it was a real anger we shared.

Midstream in our conversation, Lloyd surprised me with the comment, "I guess the most important thing that's happened has been the relationship we have developed with you."

I asked for some clarification. He continued, "Well, you've come on us so very different from what we've been used to. Not a man of the cloth, really. We have shared a great deal, just as people. I would say you have come on as a person first, a human being second, and a minister last." "Kind of person to person," I suggested. And he continued, "That's the way I would put it. More of a person than we have been used to (from the church) in our home before. You listened to me and seemed to be able to hear what I was saying and feeling. You were on my wave length." I recognized that we had some things in common. "Perhaps that's because some of our personal experiences have been similar. The things we have shared have been roles we have both known about together." And Lloyd brought that part of our conversation to a close. "I suppose so, but at least, you've been willing to hear me and know where I'm at and I've felt good about that."

Yet, to accept and understand empathetically are not enough in themselves. There needs to be some significant reflection of those feelings and facts that have been lifted up in the conversation. The other person needs to hear for themselves the thoughts that have thus far been private in the inner sanctum of their beings. This is what is meant by significant reflection. It means to be an adequate mirror for the other, letting them see in you what is happening in them. We see in a mirror dimly in the beginning of our human interchange, but then face to face as this intimate conversation begins to unfold. Since we have been accepted and know ourselves to be understood, we can then begin to recognize and embrace the self more openly as we witness its acceptability in the mirror of the other. It is easier to see oneself whole when another reflects you in an understanding and accepting way. Pastoral conversation seeks to do this.

At some point, the evangelist-caregiver must take the risk of being a clarifier for the other. S/he needs to ask, "Is this what you want to do? Is this what you want to become? Are these the options you see before you?" The evangelist makes no decision for the other, indicates no preference. S/he only lays bare the issues, the choices, and gives permission for that choice to be made. Being a mirror to a person without identifying the alternatives which are available is clearly irresponsible for the evangelist, and uncaring for the pastoral carer.

This brings us to integration, the final tenet on Carl Rogers' list. We have been shepherd. We have attended the caught lamb in the thickets of life, and now bandaged or bound in splints we move to the recovery room where we help the person integrate the thoughts, insights and decisions into the concrete actualities of their lives. We help them to look long range at their life, as we pick up the binoculars earlier laid aside in Hiltner's cartoon image. We look together toward the horizons of life, the place of becoming, and move forward toward it.

The reader may well say, at this point, What's new? This is just solid pastoral care. Perhaps true. But let's look a bit around the bend... and continue to look deeper as we listen to the further unfolding of the stories we lived with in the first part of this book.

Pastors see themselves primarily, to this point, as shepherds kneeling beside the caught lambs with the symbols of modern aid close by. They also know themselves as ones who live under the whole mandate of the gospel which calls them to preach, baptize and nourish in faith — even to nourish those whose faith is little and who practice it outside the church. They know themselves to be servants of the Christ who has a prophetic mandate to fulfill. Theirs is the task of summons and call so that the caught lambs may find themselves liberated for the full life in Christ.

Pastoral life, for clergy or lay person alike, is more than just caring. Real caring is evangelical caring! It is here that I find another of the cartoon images of Seward Hiltner to be useful. This image sees the pastor-evangelist seated, with a translator nearby, in a small group engaged in conversation. The situation is non-threatening; no pressure is evident on the faces of any of the partners in conversation. The pastor-evangelist's hands are open by way of invitation and sharing. The cross on a lapel indicates that it is the Gospel that the pastor is inviting fellow participants to consider.

The mandate is not only to heal, sustain and guide. It is also a summons and call to Christ as the source of the fullness of life. "I have come that they might have life, life in all its fullness'' is the arrogance of the evangelist's claim. S/he is about invitational caring, invitational evangelization. So while the pastor affirms that reconciliation to one's brother and sister is of the essence for humanity, the evangelist believes that reconciliation with God as we understand God in Christ is a further step toward wholeness.

The evangelizer, who is not in conflict with the principles of pastoral conversation as we have already identified them, is the one who helps others see their life in God's light while also serving the concrete needs of their human journey. They need, indeed, to be attentive to what the other is saying about their life. Yet, they also want to lead them further into considering how that need might be dealt with in the economy of the Divine. They want to invite them to try living under the reign of God, as the only truly human way of living and becoming.

The inherent danger in the pastor becoming evangelizer is that the person in need may be manipulated in the good intent of ensuring their living under the reign of God. Ends do not justify means in evangelization. Manipulation is not adequate pastoral care, nor is it permissible even in inviting people to live in the kingdom of God, or come back to church. The good shepherd is no longer good, nor the evangelizer a person of good news!

Harry Emerson Fosdick used to speak about circumnavigating the island before deciding where to land. Indeed, for the pastor-evangelist there is much to be said for discovering the whole of the person in an accepting-responding-clarifying conversation before considering the risk of landing anywhere. The right to land can only be earned after one has paid the price of attentiveness in adequate pastoral caring. The evangelist cannot be evangelist without first being caregiver.

It is impossible to become all the above in the stereotypical role of the evangelist. The proclaimer, who tells good news from six feet above comprehension and contradiction, cannot be the listening-responding- caring image of God they may so want to be, when they are by definition always from somewhere else. Do you ever wonder why so few evangelists smile? It is because they are in such a tough and impossible business. Far better to be the pastor who is part of people's ongoing lives, and better still to be the lay evangelizer who is friend or relative to the one for whom s/he wishes to be the Christian story.

If you think I have a prejudice in favor of the local homegrown evangelizer, you are quite correct. Being on the doorstep of another's life gives one a decided advantage in evangelization. It remains only to see how we can do so creatively... and easily.

CHAPTER XI
THE PHASES OF
PASTORAL CONVERSATION

Timothy was just beginning his career in ministry. He was full of enthusiasm, but short on experience. He had the potential to be good news to struggling young Christians in the early church, or he could wreak havoc in their developing lives by his excessive enthusiasm. He was like many young pastors let loose on fledgling congregations, thinking they have all the answers to life's dilemmas after a short time in seminary. That is also like recently converted Christians, filled with enthusiasm, sure they have the remedy for the human predicament that was undiscovered until their recent filling with the spirit of God. Both are dangerous to the destiny of the church, and hold back the fullness of the kingdom in other's lives.

Luckily Timothy had a wise teacher and friend. The Apostle Paul nurtured him into the disciplined disciple he was capable of becoming. That is what the two letters to Timothy are about, encouragement in becoming an evangelizer. Paul called the young pastor-evangelist to give particular attention to the wholeness of the pastoral task. He pointed out that one cannot be a good pastoral carer and neglect the mandate to share the Good News of Jesus Christ. There is a necessary link between the two in the wholeness of ministry. To share Good News is to be the evangelizer, and to complete the caring of pastoral ministry. It is to care enough! So Paul directs him: "As for you, always be steadfast, endure suffering, do the work of an evangelist, fulfill your ministry." (II Timothy 4:5)

Ultimately, the work of the evangelist is to bring another to the healing, saving, growing knowledge of Jesus Christ. It is to assist the other in accepting the invitation to join the journey of discipleship. It is to encourage the acceptance of life as a process of becoming. For that process to happen in the context of pastoral conversation, attention must be given to the principles of pastoral conversation and evangelism which have been pointed to in the previous chapters.

This very lengthy chapter, which continues the stories of those who dropped out on their journey of Dropping Back In, looks at the necessary connecting links between total pastoral caring and an evangelism which is caring. If you will, this is a thesis about pastoral evangelism.

This typology of pastoral evangelism points to six phases in pastoral conversation. My conversations with the original research sample at Harmony Church gave me many significant clues into the nature of this form of evangelical caring. My continuing journey with many more dropouts has confirmed the merits of this original typology. As I have worked with this system over the past eight years, I have become convinced that these are necessary stages in the process of evangelistic conversation. Not only are they all necessary, but they are necessary in this sequence.

It is not, however, a simple progression, of step one, step two and so one. Sometimes, conversation seems like a slippery slope. You move from one step up to the next (one phase to a second more developed phase), only to find that you are slipping back to that earlier phase. It can be up and down the ladder of human relationship. I want to indicate, however, that all of these phases are necessary phases. And all of them need to be followed one after the other. If I were to draw Turner's Phases, with that slippery slope beside it, it would look something like this:

Look with me now at these phases, in sequence, as we return to the stories of the Banyons, Marlene and others. These may help us all identify the elements in those personal relationships which lead to deeper commitment to Jesus Christ and God's Church. Perhaps it will help us see the ways we already are — or can become — "bridges of God" for those for whom we have special Christian concern.

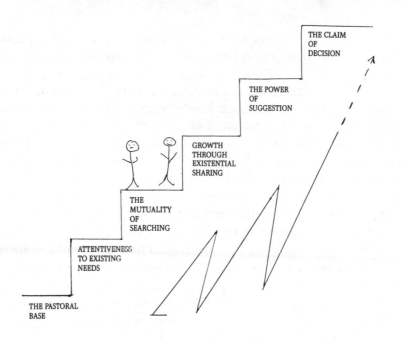

PHASE I: THE PASTORAL BASE

If pastoral conversation is to become more than caring and is to help the other person to make some gains in faith, an adequate pastoral base is absolutely essential. This phase represents, at least, being attentive to the presenting life situation of the other. It is to be the shepherd tending the caught lamb in the thickets of life with all the modern skills at his/her command. It is to live out that cartoon image of Seward Hiltner.

The pastoral base is pastoral caring. It is accepting the other for who they are, and where they are in their life's journey, without evaluating and criticizing. It is to seek to be an understanding presence of Christ to them as they are today.

Easier said than done? Of course! I was helped, some few years ago, when General Motors produced a audiovisual training tape and shared it with some of us in ministry for comments. It was titled "What you are now, is where you were when". The title says it all! One is who one is, and where one is, by grace. Of our life circumstances, many are given, few are chosen. Where I am now, and what I am now, is a product of my years of journeying through the wilderness of life. I did not set out the paths, create the maps, develop the marker points. If I had, I would likely be much more worse off than I am.

Let me tell a bit about myself. At the age of one month I was adopted into a tremendous Protestant Christian family in Montreal. I was not consulted about that. My vote didn't count. Yet, I was graced with two beautiful parents who are largely responsible for who I am today. One nurtured in me of healthy ambition and taught me the discipline of paying the price for achievement. The other taught me the quiet gift of faith, a faith that has nurtured me through some deep valleys. They were a family who went to church, for whom the Christian life was as essential as eating and breathing. They dunked me in the waters of baptism, claiming Christ for me and me for Christ. Again, they didn't ask my permission.

I grew up in a comfortable community. My family were able to help me get a university education. And my life was graced by many of their friends and acquaintances who gave me a sensitivity to many global concerns. I was privileged to live in the Province of Quebec. I could not help but learn that everyone was not like me, didn't talk like my family, and that the human fabric was enriched by our differences from our francophone neighbours.

I have a friend whose name is Frankie. He is six feet three inches tall, 250-plus pounds of muscle, and has fiery red hair. He was an inmate at the Boys' Farm and Training School some years earlier when I was the chaplain and psychologist. We became close friends.

Many times I had looked out my office window at the school and watched Frankie rumble along. He walked as if he were always mad at the world, as if it had something coming to it at the end of his fist. And so often, I said to myself, and meant it, "There but for the grace of God go I." He had been orphaned at age four. Lots of foster homes. Kicked out of every school he'd been part of. In and out of jail many times. When I met him he was only 16. Later he would tell me that I was the only family he had ever known.

Today he is a free man. He has been on the outside looking in — that is, outside of jail — for some 20 years. And perhaps grace has been part of his new-found freedom. He has yet to drop into the community of faith!

A long biographical footnote. But in the interests of underlining the fact that what I am now is where I was when, it is perhaps a useful illustration. When one begins to see the place of the other as a right place, an appropriate place for them to be, then one has a beginning sense of what that pastoral base is all about.

In terms of the conversational idiom we have referred to earlier (Carl Rogers' five tenets)) it means the accepting-understanding clarifying-integrating continuum that is fundamental to good pastoral caring. It is also what the Ethiopian eunuch experienced when Phillip "beginning with this scripture told him the good news of Jesus". (Acts 8:35)

Remember Marlene? She became a church dropout because of a crisis of faith. Her story, as we pick it up again, indicates the importance of setting an adequate pastoral base. We recall her as a person with extreme depression who was under the care of a psychiatrist. She had not been outside her house for almost five years.

I accepted readily, if not with some personal pain, her right to be who she was. That meant affirming her relationship with her father, even though it had decidedly neurotic features. I focused on the compliment it was to her father as the primary significant other in her world. When she raised the issue of sin and sickness, in a world created by a good God, I responded, "You find it hard to believe that a good God can let people suffer?" No sermonizing. No defensive reaction to shore up the credibility of God!

Our second conversation illustrates the principle of acceptance. Marlene viewed her life experience as being part of the bad news that permeates much of life, and I accepted her view as being accurate and appropriate for her.

The conversation went like this:

Marlene: ...but what do you make about all this turmoil that's going on? And the kind of trouble I had with my father?

Turner: Well, I certainly gained the impression that you've experienced more of bad news than you have of good news.....that your whole life seems to have had many negative experiences in it. And I sense that has coloured much of your reaction to God and the church.

Marlene: Well, it seems to me that when God made the world, He sure made something that got into a heck of a mess. You know, if I had been Him, and I had created the flood, one thing I would have done differently; I wouldn't have created an ark. That way the whole shooting match would have been over with and I guess he could have started again. I don't know why He saved a few of those people to go on into a world where there would be more suffering and evil.....like going from bad to worse.

Turner: That thought of in keeping with what you said last time about God not caring about the world.

Our conversation allowed Marlene to be a person with her own views about life, without condemnation or criticism. That seemed to free her to accept herself more readily than she had done previously. Not only her feelings but also her problems were accepted as being real. If I had challenged these, rather than accepting them, I have a hunch our pastoral conversations would have been soon over.

Indeed the recognition that "what I am now is where I was when" is what the pastoral base is all about. If we cannot accept others for who they are and where they are in their faith journey or life journey, then we are not fit candidates for pursuing pastoral conversation. Through us, God is unlikely to convert anyone, nor are we likely to help others grow toward an owned faith. We had better leave the church dropout alone!

However, if we have the innate human gift that finds other persons interesting simply because they are human; if we find people non-threatening whose opinions are radically different from our own; then we are good candidates for the journey beginning with the pastoral base. It is also a plus if we understand theologically that God has been part of their journey whether they recognize God or not. As someone recently said, "God's footprints are on your back whether you know it or not."

PHASE 2: ATTENTIVENESS TO EXISTING NEEDS

The Sri Lankan Christian, D.T. Niles, is often quoted as defining evangelism as one hungry beggar telling another hungry beggar where to find food. He is indeed accurate in defining this second stage of pastoral conversation. It focuses upon the presenting need at any particular time. There is little point in presenting Jesus as the bread of life to one whose belly is crying out for physical bread. Living in a poor country, Niles knew from personal experience as an evangelist that one must feed the hungry before one dare expect them to hear the Gospel of Jesus as good news.

Attentiveness to existing needs is fundamental to creative engagement in evangelistic sharing. The evidence would suggest that where needs are openly and honestly dealt with, persons are ready to let the evangelizers begin sharing their faith with them. The attempt must be honest, but not necessarily successful. We cannot meet all needs, and some may even be inappropriate to meet. But we need to make serious attempts to be helpful. The need may be practical, such as food and lodging, or it might be spiritual, focused on the search for meaning and purpose in life. It may be emotional distress, in which the human cry is for another to stand by them.

Our biblical example of the Ethiopian and Philip sheds some light for us. Philip approaches the road to Gaza as a response to a divine insight. He knows that, for some reason, he ought to be about the business of ministry on that dangerous desert road. "The Lord said to Philip, 'Rise and go toward the south to the road that goes down from Jerusalem to Gaza.' " There he meets the august treasurer of the Queen Candace riding alone in his chariot. He jogs along for a space, long enough to discover that this man is searching the Scriptures, searching for meaning, amidst a life of meaninglessness as a eunuch. Philip listens. He probably asks the eunuch some questions about the text. And then the eunuch asks his own poignant question.

Note that Philip did not begin at some predetermined point with the vulnerable and need-filled eunuch. The phrase, "beginning with this Scripture", focuses our attention on the fact that he started where the eunuch was. Only later did he move to offer some meanings for the vacuum of his life. He began at the point of need of the other.

The needs of people in conversation are not always this apparent. We seldom knock on the door of a church dropout to find them greeting us with Bible in hand and a ready question about meaning. But the truth remains. If we are attentive, if we stay with them long enough on their human journey, if we listen deeply "to the other side of me", we will discover needs in abundance. Such is the gracefilled opportunity of the evangelizer in conversation. If, however, we ride roughshod over the other person's needs, or fail to recognize them, in most cases evangelization is not welcomed. Small wonder. We then become the source of the self-fulfilling prophecy that "they didn't want to hear the good news of Jesus anyway."

Lloyd and Karen Banyon dropped out of the church because of the death of their son and a church that was unable to minister to their grief appropriately. It had become a deep seated grief of some 17 years when I first met them, and a deeply embedded anger.

Our initial conversation was courteous, somewhat superficial. They indicated how nice it was to see a minister in their home. It had been a long time. As the conversation unfolded, and they told me the story of Ron's untimely death, I sensed that their life in the last 17 years had been almost entirely focused on that loss. They kept coming back to it and I encouraged them to tell me about it. I acknowledged that Lloyd was having a particularly difficult time talking about Ron's death. I also had a deep pastoral hunch that their anger now — toward the church as "useless" and God as "angry" — was tied into the sense of inappropriate pastoral ministry at the time of the death. There was incongruence as Lloyd talked about Pastor X being a "very caring man" and God as "a guy who didn't give a damn". Anger often gets transferred to inappropriate places and persons, with the passage of time, where it can more safely be lived with.

In this initial conversation, the inappropriate behaviour of the pastor was not identified directly. Not by me, in any case. As they began to feel it a bit, I merely encouraged it to come to the surface. The Banyons did not easily acknowledge anger within themselves. Our conversation follows:

Turner: I also noticed that you kind of twigged when I mentioned his (the other minister's) name. You began to say something and then Lloyd stopped you. Was Mr X helpful to you at this time?

Karen: Well, I can't blame the man. I was in the Friendly Circle and took part in all those kinds of activities. And a fair bit of church life. But...

Lloyd: Ron was involved in the Sunday School classes as were our other two children. He had just been confirmed and he was going to church regularly.

Karen: Several nights after he went into the coma, I asked Mr. X to go and say a prayer with us around Ron's bed.

Turner: And did he go?

Karen: Yes, he did go, but then we never saw him again after the funeral. I kind of hoped he might come over and share some of his feelings with us while we were going through this agony.

Turner: You felt letdown that he didn't come and share some of the pain with you.

Karen: Well, I guess you could put it that way. I didn't have any right to expect it, but I did hope he would share a little bit of what we were going through.

Turner: And Mr X. took the funeral when Ron died?

Karen: Yes.

Turner: Did he not come around after the funeral to be with you then?

Karen: Oh, after a very long time he came back. He didn't have all that much helpful stuff to say to us. I guess not every minister does.

Turner: You felt let down by your minister when you really needed him.

Karen: I guess you could put it that way...

That gentle acknowledgement of what was a torrent of feeling did something inside them during the following week. When I came back, they were soon into a tirade about the inappropriate ministry they had received and the "failure of the church to us". A gush of emotion surfaced in our two hour conversation. It had been steaming for years. But this gentle permission to talk about their need to be angry also allowed them to begin the process of disengaging their anger from God and placing it more appropriately where it belonged. Later this would help them to begin to look at the church as a renewed option they could consider with integrity.

I suspect that if I had been more aggressive in pursuing

this need, I would have failed in these conversational encounters. If I had aggressively gone after this feeling of anger, even identified it by name, it might have had a deleterious effect. On the other hand, if I had been defensive about the pastoral pressures of ministry and tried to justify the pastor's actions, in the hope of comforting them, it would have been experienced as false comfort. They might well have displaced this anger onto me, as the "representative minister", and not been open to a deeper engagement with Christ or the Church.

Their anger was indeed justified. They were encouraged to engage it and mobilize it to the full, in the service of their becoming more fully human. I listened and encouraged that need to be brought forward so it could be met in mutual conversation and grief sharing.

Mrs. Kong was quite a different case. She was a second generation Canadian who had left the church some five years earlier. She had a commanding presence in the doorway when she greeted me. When she discovered my mission, she indicated quickly that she had no personal need to see me but that a neighbour was in desperate need. Would I go across the road and see her? But she herself did not need my ministry, at this moment and probably never.

She told me a bit about her neighbour. Her husband had died six months previously, had been buried by a family friend who was an Army chaplain. Her 20-year-old son was giving her problems. Repeatedly he was being brought home drunk. The tragedy was that he was a college student and before his Father's death had done well academically. Could I please help her friend?

So I went across the street. True to the story, there was abundant need in that other home. Since it would not serve any purpose of this book to tell their story, let me simply indicate that the resources of the community were mobilized in the interests of that family. The story did have a happy ending.

Having done what Mrs Kong asked, and having responded to her presenting need, I returned to see her. What need? The need was obviously to get rid of me! She didn't want me close to her and her own tragic story. So, since I had done what she asked, I wandered by days later, and thanked her on behalf of the neighbour family for "your ministry to them". She laughed a bit, and then reluctantly invited me in.

Later she would tell me the story of the tragic death of her husband, a death she could not talk about, a suicide. I sensed that the only way she could deal with the guilt she felt for his death was by keeping people at a distance. I will never forget that imposing picture: an Oriental matriarch, arms crossed over her breasts, clearly saying, "I'm too afraid to let you close to me for you may discover the guilt only God knows about."

It's good to remember our pastoral failures, as well as successes. It keeps us appropriately human. I remember Alice whom I met in hospital during her surgery for a radical mastectomy. Because she was on the outside looking in, and had formerly been in the choir at Harmony, I decided to do some follow-up care when she returned home. We met several times during her recuperation, which was lengthy. She died 18 months later, never having shown any interest in returning to the church. The following conversation may indicate why.

We talked about the reluctance she was feeling in the relationship with the medical personnel at the cancer treatment centre.

Turner: So you don't feel you were dealt with as a person?

Alice: Well, not exactly. The doctors were good enough when they talked to you in the interviews, but they didn't answer any more questions than you asked. They didn't tell you much about what was going on and I had very little to do with the nurses or the therapists, so I didn't learn very much.

Turner: You would have liked them to be more straightforward with you?

Alice: I guess that's how you would put it. I would like them to have told me more, anyway. I want to understand more of what I've been going through.

Turner: Alice, I've been wondering about something else as well. You know, with all this crisis you have been through, I've been wondering if your faith has been of any support and value to you?

Alice: (as tears begin to come to her eyes) Yes, I can say

that my faith has been of some help (as more tears start to well up).

Turner: Well, what I've been thinking is that you are a person with a great faith background. Most of your faith has been sung rather than said because of your involvement in choirs, and music seems to be important to you. I was wondering if this kind of thing comes back to you as a strength or comfort at this time.

Alice: Yes, yes. It has been of some help. It's hard to say how, but it has been a support.

Alice did get better, for a period. However, I always lived with the suspicion that her faith was only of "some help". Her hurried, almost emphatic "yes, yes" indicate in retrospect that she was pleading for me to respond at a totally different level than I did. Perhaps it would have been more appropriate to ask about the nature of her tears or to reflect her comment on "some help". We always ask perhaps in retrospect. Her need for meaning and purpose, a firm faith foundation on which she could stand in tough times, was not something I was able to nurture in our pastoral conversations. Her deepest needs went unmet. And at her funeral I shed more than one tear.

If I could rerun some of that conversation I might do it differently. Like this: "Alice, I see it is difficult for you to talk about what your faith means to you. Can you help me understand why it is difficult?" This might have freed her to admit that her resources of faith had not met the test, that she needed help spiritually to go on, or that she was really feeling fearful about what the future held in store for her. These possibilities, at least, lurk in the darkness of those tears. Her real needs, I suspect, were never identified to me or her doctors. If they had been, we might well have seen her back in Church before she died.

Hence the bottom line: where presenting needs are articulated and met, at least in part, progress can be made toward the goal of evangelization. Permission is granted by the other to proceed in conversation or with our relationship when we have genuinely been helpful to them. Where these needs are skirted or not identified properly, there seem to be blocks to the pastoral evangelization.

It is always a matter of "seeing what's on the other side

of me, the side of me that reaches out to you." That indeed is the privilege of pastoral conversation.

PHASE 3: THE MUTUALITY OF SEARCHING

The human journey is often a long, winding and lonely road. We do not, by nature, wish to make that journey alone. Hence we invite others to take away the lonesomeness of our solitary journey and make it into a shared discovery. That is what marriage is about. Partnerships in business witness to taking shared risks. Coalitions, of one nature or another, give us solidarity to face the threats of life.

The third phase in pastoral conversation is called the mutuality of searching. It gives credence to the Christ statement, and human affirmation, that where two or three are together in the name of Christ there Christ is in the midst of the community. Seldom does he meet us on a solitary walk.

I find the Biblical model, to which we have made continuing reference, helpful in understanding this phase. We last saw Philip engaged in conversation with the eunuch of Ethiopia, searching the Scriptures for meaning and purpose concerning his life. Philip, the evangelizer, had appropriately "begun where he was", with his question, with his point of need. One can see this faithful servant of God moving tirelessly along beside the carriage, hanging in with the conversation. The Ethopian was "seated in his chariot", but invited Philip to come up into the carriage and continue the journey seated beside him.

It is when the journey is made mutual, by the invitation of the listener, that the mutuality of searching happens. It is at this point that the encounter ceases to be solely pastoral caring and moves toward evangelization. This indeed is one of the creative turning points in what I call pastoral conversation. The Ethiopian and Philip have become a twosome in pursuit of discoveries for both of their lives. Not only might the Ethiopian's life be opened to new discoveries, so will the evangelizer Philip's. Journeying in faith makes both vulnerable to the discoveries of faith, as we are apprehended by the God who first discovers us.

Let us return to the story of Marlene. Some excerpts

from her case file indicate where mutuality in searching led to some growth in both persons. In our second conversation, we are both engaged in a search for God's credibility in an incredible world. It went like this:

Turner: That thought is kind of in keeping with the thought you shared last time about God not caring about His world.

Marlene: Well, I feel that way. I don't think God really cares about what He's created. Why else would He have let my father suffer so much?

Turner: It doesn't seem very fair to you.

Marlene: No. I guess that's why there should be a heaven... to make things more equal than they are here. At least that may make up for all this suffering. But anyway, it doesn't make sense to me. Does it make any sense to you?

Turner: Well, much of the world we experience seems to make a lot of nonsense. At least, when we look at it from our usual perspective. I guess what you're saying really is that God is out of control in this world.

Marlene: I guess that's really what I mean. Like, he doesn't seem to care or He doesn't want to. I really don't know what to make of it all. In some ways I have become very bitter about this whole experience.

Turner: I sense that even in your present circumstances that it is impotant for you to believe that God is in control.

Marlene: Well, I wish He was, but He isn't.

Turner: You'd like to believe, though, that He is, wouldn't you?

Marlene: Of course, I would but I know that my life has been such of a piece that He doesn't care!

Our conversation that day began with our consideration of God's supposed control of our life and the need to find that to be true in this present moment of Marlene's life. Later in that conversation we bantered back and forth about the possibility of Christ as Victor. We mused some more on the relationship between sin and freewill. A week later we focused on whether hope might be just an illusion or might possibly be something integral to the Christian lifestyle. It was heavy stuff. And she seemed always to set the agenda.

In the last of our four interviews, Marlene began to

show some tremendous strides toward integrating the theological convictions of Christian hope into the fabric of a newly acquired optimism for her life. The mutuality of our search after the credibility of God had found a new seedbed rooted in a more secure feeling of self-worth. Her psychiatrist was genuinely surprised with what was happening in her life. He called and asked that I continue seeing her past this research phase. I did so with pleasure. Marlene continues to be a good friend and although she still fears the outside world we do have the occasional golf game together.

Marlene had moved from a high degree of outright hostility to God to being able to see herself in God's image. She began to gain glimpses of herself as worthwhile, perhaps one who might even have a contribution to make in the economy of the Commonwealth of God.

And this mutual journey, what did it do for me? It was certainly one of the more human encounters I have had with church dropouts. It made me recognize my own humanity more, and my continuing struggles around the issue of good and evil. We still laugh when we talk about God having some answers to give us about what's happened in our lives. But most of all, it confirmed for me that evangelization is really about incarnational presence. It confirmed for me that, what I had oftimes said in lectures was true. "Evangelization is to be the Christian story, to do the Christian story, and to tell the Christian story." I had done that for Marlene. She had also done it for me. In our tears and laughter we had been grace to each other. We had been in mutual ministry.

Sometimes the mutuality of searching happens most readily because we have parallel life journeys. Such was the case with the Banyons.

Once Lloyd and Karen had ventilated their rightful anger concerning the pastor who was absent when they needed him, they were free to deal with the primary concern of their past 17 years. It was necessary, but not easy, to talk through the many and complex feelings they had about their son's untimely death. They had a lot of residual guilt about his being alone in his bedroom when he went into the coma, and a lot of what if questions surrounding whether they had not been observant enough to notice warning signs of impending doom.

though the doctors had confirmed that there was nothing they could have done earlier, it had not assuaged their guilt.

By the third interview, the Banyons, like the eunuch, had somehow decided they did not want to continue the journey alone. They wanted a fellow traveller, one who might have travelled some of the side roads they thought were unique to their journey. They suspected that a pastoral minister might have been down some of their blind alleys with others before them. But none of us were expecting what happened later that night. That story remains to be told, however, in the next phase.

Because I had been there when they let go of their anger at that former pastor, it seemed I earned my entry into their lives. After that it was much more relaxed. We could share their disappointment also in the other people of the church who wouldn't talk about Ron after his death. We don't talk easily about pain. And death. And divorce. And all the other supposed failures in our lives. We like to talk about nice things. Hence the Banyons were left alone in grief by lay people in the congregation as well. They cared, but they couldn't endure the pain of listening too deeply! Not just those who wear the title "Reverend", but all persons in the church are called to be in ministry! That is the message of the final chapters of this book.

They wondered why we talked so easily about their pain and turmoil. Why did it drew a ready tear from my eyes as well as their own? They suspected that it might be because I had been a pastor for some years and had been with many families in bereavement. Soon they were to sense that our journey was deeply mutual because of another painful fact. Indeed they had already sensed that they were in ministry to/ with me. They wouldn't have used that term, but they sensed the draw of caring from them to me. They were givers as well as receivers.

Then toward the end of that evening it dawned on them that our journeys might be the same. Could my feelings have been based on my own life's experience? They were not about to reveal their hunch that night. After checking it out with some people in the church, they put it forward during our next conversation. "Is it true that you also.....?"

When the journey has become mutual, it has potential

to go much deeper. It can become a rich seedbed for growth and nourishment for both travellers. The journey of the discovery of faith is enabled to move forward in creatively fresh ways. One can thus become the channel of God's grace that leads to conversion.

But you don't get here without having been there! The invitation to mutuality only happens after one has been attentive to existing needs within the context of a pastoral base that believes others are "what I am now is where I was when".

PHASE 4: GROWTH THROUGH EXISTENTIAL SHARING

The Christian evangelizer is in the "becoming" business! People can best become whom they are called to become under God when the stuff of their lives touches creatively the stuff of another person's life in such a way that the Incarnation happens all over again. God, in fact, becomes flesh again!

Let me tell you about the triangle of faith. It will help us understand better why faith happens for some people, and appears to be an impossibility for others.

The triangle of faith is based upon my understanding of faith as "story". Faith sharing is the sharing of stories. In this triangle there are three corners, representing three particular stories.

The top corner of the triangle represents *the* story. This is the story of God dancing through the lines of human history, particularly in the history of the chosen people, Israel, and in the people of the New Testament Church. It is centred in the person and work of Jesus whom we call the Christ. It is always God revealing God's self in the story, the journey, of history. Theologians have often referred to this as "salvation history". Our German theological friends have coined that beautiful word "heilegeschichte".

The God story is what is contained in the Old and New Testaments. It is what I am fond of calling the Christian Story. It is that which we own as Christians when we hold in our believing hearts the old and new covenants. When Billy Graham, or any other revivalists, mention that "the Bible says" it is to this recorded, inspired, formative witness that they are pointing.

This is the story that we come to celebrate in worship, whether in word or sacrament. It is that story which forms us in our Christian nurture as adults and youth. Out of this story we are compelled to "do justly and love mercy" and are pushed into our work in the global village. It is our story! We live out of it, are formed by it. It is the central drama of our beings as Christians.

The bottom left corner is *my* story. This is the story of my faith journey, how the God of Jesus Christ has danced on the lines of my life. It is that story of "what I am now is where I was when". For me, that journey is appropriately sacred ground.

No two stories are alike. Because Christian commitment is about a personal relationship to Jesus Christ, they must all be different. Sameness is for the General Motors production line. So faith journeys are to be celebrated; they are to be affirmed; they are to be told. And none is more important, or significant, than the other. Not Mother Teresa. Not Jean Vanier. Not Lois Wilson or John Wesley. Not your story or my story either. All are important parts of the fabric of God continuing to make history.

The bottom right hand corner of this faith triangle represents the *other's* story. This is the one with whom we are engaged in pastoral conversation. It is that person of faith or non-faith with whom we are talking. It could be Marlene or the Banyons.

Whether they are aware of it or not, they are persons with a a story, a faith story. It matters not whether they have experienced God, God has experienced them on their journeys. God is always the "God with us". As my Newfoundland friend put it, "God has his footprints all over you, mate." So, their stories also are sacred ground. They are stories to be respected and listened to. They have the right to be where they are in faith. It has been their journey with God up to this point.

These three corners represent the "why" of faith. There is *the* story, *my* story, and the *other's* story. Why faith happens appears to be related to the interconnectedness of these three stories.

I like to put the happening of faith like this: when your story bends towards my story, and God's story bends towards both our stories, we can (both) dare to believe. The leap of faith happens most easily when my story is touched by your story, and both our stories are touched by God's story. Faith happens, indeed, in an incarnational way. As it happened in and through Jesus touching the lives of others, so today it happens most often through the human agency of person-to-person touching. It is being the Christian story for each other.

Perhaps if we can pick up the conversation with Lloyd and Karen Banyon where we left off, it will illustrate in a helpful way both the faith triangle and growth through existential sharing. You will remember that we left them with Lloyd thinking through some possibilities of what might have happened in my own life journey. In retrospect it seems as if he had to check those hunches before daring to raise them. After some checking, he plunged forthrightly into our next conversation. It would prove to be both painful and helpful to us all.

I entered their home for what was supposed to be the fourth and final interview in the research process. It led to

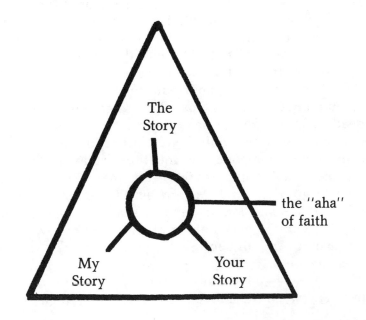

many more, and deeper, conversations over the months ahead. As I began to sit down, she blurted out, "Is it true, Gord, that you also lost a son... that you had a son who died?" I literally collapsed into the easy chair and knew that I was in for a tough evening. It would be tough on me, even if not on them. I replied, "Yes, that's true."

So began a long evening of two stories bending toward each other. It was an evening often punctuated by tears, and bitter thoughts, and angry affirmations. "Were you angry with God?" "Did you want to leave the church?" "Did you leave it?" "What about the minister who buried your son, did he come back?" (The parallel was strange; that pastor never came back inside our door either.) "And others in the church, did they avoid you too... and your grief?" (And yes, they also had vanished from their usual caring ministry.)

I didn't have to look very far for parallels. Our stories bent toward each other time and again that night, and in the nights that ensued. I knew what it was to feel forsaken by God. I'd heard all the answers in seminary, but now they didn't seem to add up to much. I knew what it was like to feel helplessly alone in the community called church. I've never been sure why I stayed with the church. Others in my situation, like the Banyons, often leave the church forever.

It was a long night. Lots of tears. Lots of anger and bitterness. Both theirs and mine. And just a bit of hope!

As we came to the close of that evening, we found that *the* story — the God story — was also strangely, yet wonderfully, bending toward both our stories. We both alluded to it several times. God was One who also gave up a beloved son to death on a cross. And wasn't there a story in the Old Testament of a father who was willing to sacrifice his son on the altar of a mountain? Someone also mentioned that the father, in the parable of the Waiting Father, gave the younger son the freedom to go away and destroy his life. Over the weeks that followed we had lots of time to share in what those stories might say to the very human predicament that we now knew we shared. And all because Lloyd dared to ask "Has you life been like ours?"

I have spent many hours trying to analyse what happened between the Banyons and myself that night. Certainly it was the creative edge of new beginnings of faith for me. It was also a faith nurturing experience for them. It was the beginning of their "dropping back in" to the church. They came the following Sunday, much to my surprise.

During the past few years my favourite spiritual mentor has been Henri Nouwen. I read almost everything he wrote. He spoke to me in a private and encouraging way. One day Seward Hiltner asked me if I had read one of his books called *The Wounded Healer.* I hadn't. Hiltner indicated it might add something creative to my understanding of pastoral conversation. So I began to read. He said what I was feeling. He put in words what I believe is the essence of ministry and surely the crux of creative pastoral conversation.

Nouwen indicated that the real power of our ministry does not come from our humanly defined strengths but rather from our apparent human weaknesses. What the world counts weak, God counts as strength. It is those "wounds which by God's grace have been healed" which are the real strengths we have to offer to others in pastoral and evangelical ministry.

Let me say a word about those wounds. First, they come in all kinds and shapes. They are never identical. They are only parallel. They are the woundedness of losing a child to death, a parent to the grave, a spouse at an earlier-than-expected time. They are the woundedness of divorce, job loss, personal failure, imprisonment, mental illness. Second, they are not the gift of God. Most often they are the tragic unexplained circumstances of one's life journey. Third, there is no grace to be received from fresh wounds that are still oozing and merely add to the woundedness of others. Nouwen means the wounds that have been healed, by the grace of God. So, fourth they are the strong scar tissue of one's spiritual journeying. "By his wounds are we healed" is as true of the Messiah as it is of those who practice the wounded healer ministry of evangelization.

Only as those whose wounds have healed begin to minister to the wounds of another which are still raw, do they see the gift in their own woundedness. They need not accept that heretical theology which affirms their brokenness as being a gift of God. But they do grow in a faith that God can reweave the broken fabric of wounded lives into glorious tapestries of useful ministry. In this can God's glory be proclaimed in fresh and creative ways. They come to be grateful that their brokenness can be helpful to others. Their wounds become lessened as they continue the journey of the wounded healer.

I don't know how much you can let your imagination grow into the story of the Ethiopian eunuch. For me, the story is not complete in its telling. I suspect that there was some parallel brokenness in the life of Philip. The eunuch wondered about the possibility of baptism. Could Philip perhaps — perhaps — have talked about the "washing of baptism" in his own life? Might he have shared the story of his incorporation into the community of Christ's faithful people as a way he had found meaning and purpose for his life? And might he have talked about the ups and downs of that journey? I wonder. But I suspect that somehow his story bent towards the eunuch's story (and vice versa). And perhaps both of their stories were touched by God's story. For indeed, they both took the risk to believe. Both became evangelizers!

It was so also with Marlene. Our struggles for integrity in life were not the same but they had some strange and creative touching points. She had an intuitive hunch that I knew something at a much deeper level about what she was suffering. She reached to pull that story from within me, almost in a demanding way in our second conversation. "I wonder if your life has been all sweetness and roses? I'll bet there are some rough edges you've been over too, in terms of your faith." As already indicated I had lost a child at birth. This different experience of woundedness would be used later to share the pain which we had in common in the human community of caring. I would become a "wounded healer" to Marlene in a different way than I could be to the Banyons.

Turner: ....you seem to feel that if one believes in God everything will turn out all right and our lives should be success stories.

Marlene: Isn't that the way it's supposed to be?

Turner: Well, I think of the first funeral I had to take when I came to Harmony. It was the funeral of my closest friend.

Marlene: Oh, yes, I remember. The young teacher.

Turner: He was a classmate of mine, 32 years old and

he died of brain cancer. I watched him die bit by bit in the hospital. It was a horrible experience.

Marlene: I remember hearing about that. He was apparently an awfully fine man.

Turner: Yes, one of the best.

Marlene: Do you have a daughter?

Turner: Yes, I have a three-year-old daughter.

Marlene: Oh, that's nice. Do you have any other children?

Turner: Yes, I have an 11-year-old son.

Marlene: Oh... there's eight years between them. (A pause.)

Turner: Yes. That's part of what I meant when I said I didn't have a silver spoon in my mouth either. We had another child in between who died at birth. That was pretty difficult to accept and live with. As a matter of fact, there was a long time when I felt some of what you feel about God... anger and bitterness and fear. I think it's pretty understandable that we feel that way. But we feel as Christians, we shouldn't talk much about it.

Marlene: Well, I'm not sure we should talk about it very much. I feel very guilty about talking about my mother the way I have been. (She had earlier indicated how upset she was with her mother for mistreating the father who was "the best friend I ever had.") I haven't shared that with many people before... I guess with hardly anyone. Only my husband knows how I really feel about my mother. The doctors told me I should be able to talk to my friends or someone about what's really down deep.

Turner: Well, it's important to talk about our deep feelings. And I think its important also to talk in the church about the negative feelings we have about God.

My willingness to talk about my own anger and bitterness toward God didn't make Marlene comfortable at first. She focused her angry feelings on the relationship with her mother. Mother had become the God-figure in her life that she could rail out at. Heaven forbid that she should cast any aspersions on her father for dying! Some moments later she would return to her angry thoughts about God. A few weeks later she admitted that she wished "I could tell God to go to hell". When she was able to do that, she had moved closer to engaging her faith journey again. The god whom she told to "go to hell" was no god at all. She was beginning to be freed to embrace the God who was the real God for her.

In one of our final conversations (in this research phase) she acknowledged the central need for her to become whole again. It was a significant statement.

Marlene: I guess that makes sense. I don't know really why I lost faith or where it went to. It just evaporated.

Turner: Well, our task is to try to help you find it again, wherever it's gone.

Marlene: Yes, I guess that's the important thing, to recover it and put it back in my life.

As we continued to share the wounds of our somewhat similar life journeys, we shared often about the reality of sin, evil and free will. How tough it is to live in a world of totalitarian evil! Marlene struggled to claim some optimism that needed to be foundational for the future of her life. She noted that I had called it "hope"' and she thought that might be the central issue for her becoming a whole person. I agreed. In our final session together she indicated she was beginning to claim "new directions" for her life and that "the lights are turning on". She felt her home was no longer a vacuum and "I feel that the Almighty is really a part of my life again." As we left each other for the last time she claimed that God was more real to her now than God had been for many years. I suspect it was because we had become wounded healers to each other. The miracle of transformation had once again begun to happen.

Six months after this, Marlene moved to Calgary with her husband. She left us a happier and more whole person.

We are all wounded healers. Or can become them. We all have emotional and spiritual wounds. It is from these that we can best minister. I sincerely believe that existential sharing holds the greatest potential for us in aiding the Christian growth of others. As we tell our story and share our faith the journey of becoming happens for them and us. The mandate of evangelization happens. We are indeed enabled to "go and make disciples".

I suspect that as I have completed Marlene's story, I have hinted at what the next phases are all about. So be it!

PHASE 5: THE POWER OF SUGGESTION

The original research, since confirmed, identified something that is essential to move people to claim their faith. It is particularly significant for those who have been bruised by the church and dropped out. I refer to the power of suggestion.

The journey toward faith ownership, like any struggle that involves significant change or growth, is a lonely one. If it is possible to travel that road with another, particularly one who has given some evidence of being down that road before, then the natural human desire is to pursue that treck in company with the other. This human trait brought us to, and through, the mutuality of searching as well.

People do not make faith gains without encouragement. To risk making the faith journey a second time, having been on the outside looking in, is frightening. If, at the crucial time, something is suggested to you which seems to add credibility to some beginning faith steps you have just taken, this seems to encourage further creative bridges to that faith journey. We simply do not easily go into the dark alone. We will risk it more readily if someone suggests that we can do so. Encouragement is the power that suggests we should continue in the way we are going.

This means, of course, that one only encourages in the way that person is already going. We give them further nudges; bump them along. Never do we suggest a direction which is the opposite. For instance, if they are showing a continued resistance to church involvement because of the bruises they have had, it is entirely inappropriate — even damaging — to suggest, "Maybe you'd like to come to church with me next Sunday and see if it's different." Angry eyes don't have the ability to see things differently!

As a rule of thumb, never invite a church dropout back to church! I repeat, never invite a church dropout back to church. If you are doing your task of evangelization adequately, at the appropriate time, they will invite themselves back to church. They will ask you, "Do you think it would be all right if I came back to church?" Or, "Maybe the church has changed. Do you think it might be worth a try again?" Then, it is appropriate to "suggest" .... "I think you are wanting to try it again.

93

Sure that would be all right. And maybe it would be easier if you didn't do it alone. Would it be all right if I went along with you that first Sunday?''

Perhaps if we pick up the conversation with Marlene again, it will illustrate this. We left Marlene wondering about the possibility of building faith back into her life. She was not sure why she had lost faith. Now she was wrestling with whether a renewed faith might make her into a heathier person.

So, we pick up the conversation:

Marlene: But how do you get out of this (bind I am in)? How am I going to be become better? I don't have that much faith in psychiatry.

Turner: Well, I'm wondering if we could talk a little more about your faith. It seems to me that one of the things our faith has to say to us is about hope. It seems to me that this is the most important thing about our Christian faith and the thing that makes it different.

Marlene: I guess that's true, but I don't feel very hopeful. This world isn't a very hopeful place. We live in the midst of all this mess. Like my neighbour next door, dying of cancer, and Doug's wife down the street. She died of cancer. And you hear about children with leukemia and all those things.

Turner: The real world we live in is a small world full of problems, but I wonder what you believe about how things will turn out in the end. Do you believe that things will turn out all right?

Marlene: Now you're beginning to sound like a Seventh Day Adventist, as if things are coming to an end.

Turner: No. I don't mean that at all. I don't believe things are coming to an end very soon. What I mean is do you believe that ultimately God will have things in control?

Marlene: I don't know. I just know that things are all messed up here now and God doesn't seem to care.

Marlene certainly is teetering on the brink of new directions. Hope is a possibility, but not a live option for her. It will be a struggle for her to reinvest herself in the faith-hope journey. Yet she is clearly wanting to. And it is clearly one of the building blocks she needs to put in place if her life is going to grow toward wholeness. But she will be unable to do so without some nudge.

As our conversation closed that afternoon, I took the risk of suggesting that what she wanted to do was appropriate. "Marlene, I know you feel it would be tough to begin believing again in God and yourself. But I hear you wanting to take that step. I want you to know that I think you are already believing... at least a little bit. Maybe you ought to try it again in your own way. We can see if it stands up for you or not. I'll keep with you in the next few weeks as you try it." And then I left. When I came back a few days later, Marlene was a decidedly different woman. We had made another step along the journey of life, together!

Let's pick up the story of the Banyons again. It illustrates this phase even more markedly. There were several conversational processes which indicated the importance of the power of suggestion. The following conversation came just before they came back to the life of the church.

At this point we had dealt with their pain and anguish in the loss of Ron. We had done our crying and screaming at the pastor who had failed them and the congregation who didn't care when they could have cared. We had blamed God too. And we had come out the other side smiling. We talked about the fact that we weren't all that hot either and guessed that we might have some things to confess to God too. We admitted that we also had let friends down when they needed us. We said our goodbyes to that painful chapter in our personal life stories and determined to get on with the business of living. (We knew underneath that we would still return time and again to that painful chapter.)

Now we were ready to talk about the church again. It too wouldn't be easy. The Banyons went back to their memory that when they were inside the church they hadn't gotten much out of it anyway. A typical excuse? Yes, but needful at this juncture. There wasn't much challenge ormeaning, as they could recall it. "Would it be any different now? Was there any real point in going back?" I listened long as they talked about the-used-to-be church. I listened also as they talked about the creative edges of their life in the community. They were not idle folk, they put a lot back into the community in service and personal sacrifice. Then, I reminded them of the things they had been saying about how solid their faith had been. "We really were believing people, you know!" And I sensed the validity in what they were saying. I used this as a building block from which to move forward.

Turner: You know, from the way you have been speaking today, I have one thing I would like to throw in here.

Lloyd: What's that?

Turner: Well, I really have to say that a person with your convictions and the way you use your life shouldn't be outside the church. I really feel that you ought to be inside the church now, getting fed for the way you use your life outside.

Lloyd: Well, yes, I agree, but oh, I don't know. I guess you get out of the pattern of the thing and just don't seem to be able to get back in.

Turner: Well, I guess it's because I believe in the church... like you seem to be saying... has something to give you...

Our conversation wandered all over the terrain of the church and its life for the next while. We parted without a conclusion on the issue. But then God's conclusion is the only one that counts! And that's what we call conversion. Imagine my surprise when on Sunday they were in the 13th row from the back, left side. I had learned the power of suggestion again, as I would many more times in working with church dropouts.

I often fantasize about that story of Philip and the Ethiopian eunuch. Philip begins with the scriptural focus of the eunuch. He begins at the other's present position. And they talk, and share, and laugh, and cry. He tells the other about this Jesus who has been good news in his life. Then there is a gap in the story.

We find ourselves by a river. We find ourselves faced with a question. The other (the eunuch) asks it, not the evangelizer. "What is to prevent my being baptized?" Good question. What is there to stop those wishing to own their faith journey from owning it when they are ready to do so? But also the question needs to be asked, what made him ready to own the Christian faith at this point?

Perhaps the conversation unfolded something like this:

Philip: So, you see this Jesus has been the companion on my journey that I needed. Not that life has always been easy. We've talked about the tough times I've had too. But at least this Jesus made it manageable for me.

Ethiopian: Well, you know how tough it's been to live with this mark against my humanity. People ridicule me. They use me for their ends. I feel less than human.

Philip: I know. It can't be easy. But, still, I sense that you are attracted to this Jesus of whom I speak.

Ethiopian: That's true. He certainly is different from others of your race. Oh, different from others of any race. I find it hard though to believe that he could see something of real value in me. Or that I might have something to contribute to who he is.

Philip: Yes, that's tough to believe. But I still think that you do believe... maybe more than just a little bit.

Ethiopian: Yes, I need something more than I have. A good job and prestige are all right. But I know that there must be more to making me feel a whole person.

Philip: Could it be that this Jesus offers something you have been looking elsewhere for? Maybe your journey to Jerusalem was all about what we are talking about... meaning and wholeness.

Ethiopian: Maybe. Could it be that Jesus is that giver of meaning and purpose for me? I'm beginnning to think this is so. What is there to stop me from continuing this journey with Jesus? Could I be baptized in his name like others? In this river over there?

Life's lonely journey can go somewhere when another says it's all right to keep going in the direction you are moving. We simply are permission-givers for those who wish to claim the faith discoveries that are unfolding in their lives. And then we stand aside and let them do so.

PHASE 6: CLAIMING OUR DECISIONS FOR LIFE

One thinks of evangelization often in terms of decision. A person presents, from the pulpit or in conversation, the claims of Jesus Christ as Lord and Saviour with the expectation that the hearer will respond by making a definite decision, yes or no, for example. Billy Graham calls his television programs "The Hour of Decision".

Yet, very little is known about the nature of decisional moments. We know when people make these formidable decisions for living, yet why they make them is a mystery. Why do some accept the claims of Christ laid before them, and others reject them? Billy Graham claims not to understand it fully. Neither do I.

Mystery lies at the heart of conversion. Perhaps that is because God is essentially mystery. We see God dimly; our human experience of the other is always clouded, but then we shall see God face to face. In any case, conversion is not our business. Conversion is the mandate of God; it is the work of the Divine . Why God effects change in one person and not in the other is at the heart of the mystery. Our task, as evangelizers, is merely to be the faithful human vessels which carry the Christian story so that it has the opportunity of engaging with the present tense story of the hearer. If we are faithful in that human task, then God has the opportunity to work the miracle of human transformation we call conversion. God has chosen to make the divine interdependent on the human in the process of evangelization. Our task is key to transformation but the Transformer is still God.

In many ways this makes the task of evangelization both easier and yet more urgent. Since we no longer feel ourselves responsible for people's decisions, we lose that sense of guilt for underachieving. It becomes easier to share our faith without being offensive. We can more easily avoid the dangers of manipulation and pushiness. However, knowing the interdependence God has claimed us for, as responsible stewards of the mysteries of God we recognize the urgency of the task which is ours. No one can shirk the task of evangelizing — it belongs to all of us — since our failure to be the Christian story, when and where we can, denies others the possibility of God working the miracle of their transformation. Our task in evangelization is not only important, it is essential!

Listening to the stories of church dropouts has made me increasingly sensitive to a number of issues in the area of decisions for Christ. It has helped me consider some new possibilities for helping people live under the reign of God in Christ Jesus.

First, claiming our decisions for life is a solitary business. That does not mean it is lonely. People need to be allowed to claim their own decisions in appropriate and individual ways. We ought not to choose for them, define the decision for them, or push them into it. Premature closure of people's decisions for Christ and the church, I am sure, has left many on the doorstep of commitment rather than inside the door of the household of God. Because we are individuals, an intricate maze of needs and possibilities, and because God has chosen to relate to us personally, our manner of deciding will be individual.

It would have been inappropriate to suggest that Marlene come back to church. She probably will never be able to tolerate the closeness of community togetherness. On my last Sunday as her pastor she did struggle to come to church. She got dressed, put on a hat and headed to the corner. When she saw the steeple, she froze. She could go no further.

But Marlene did decide to become more whole. She did decide to become a hope-filled person. She did decide to struggle with the Christian journey in her own way. And she was a growing person in Christ! That is conversion! She claimed her decision for life, under God, as was appropriate for her.

The Banyons did come back to church. They returned as if they had never left. For them, it was an appropriate way in which they could re-engage their journey with this now-acceptable God. They had forgiven, and felt forgiven and renewed.

A second thing surfaces for me. Decisions are made more easily when one has a partner in that process. That other person will be largely passive, most often silent. Perhaps only a nod of the head or a raised eyebrow will indicate approval of what we are deciding. And when they have decided, perhaps our hugs or tears will indicate the sense of togetherness we have felt with them in this very privileged journey we have shared.

So, for this writer and evangelizer, pastoral evangelism is indeed about sharing and growth. "Go and make disciples" means literally to invite others to the journey of being learners in the school of Christ. It is the beckoning to becoming! Our aim is the growth of persons as individual spiritual beings under God. So we watch the freedom from bondage of a Marlene, the inclusion in community of the Banyons, and we know that they have claimed some new decisions for life. They have voted to be in Christ and to journey in the Christian way.

CHAPTER XII
IS IT WORTH IT? ASSESSING
ENGAGEMENT EVANGELIZATION

The reader will recognize that pastoral evangelism is time- consuming. The fact that persons may well decide differently than we planned also may make it frustrating and lacking in apparent rewards. Is it worth it?

Our experience with pastoral conversation with church dropouts indicates that of those who will return to the church, or re-engage with their faith journey, 50 percent will do so after our initial visit and conversation. That is, if we are able to engage with the real reason they left. For the rest, it seems that we need to visit them once for every year they have been absent from the life of the church. That means patience and persistence.

Pastoral evangelism is tough work. It means long-term commitment to healing the pain and injury which church dropouts have suffered at the hand of the church and in the storms of life.

Pastoral evangelism also means excitement. It means meaningful ministry for the whole people of God. Those who undertake it know themselves to be involved in the essence of what ministry is about and they are glad to be used in the service of Christ in this exciting way. As one of our evangelizers said after six months on our outreach team, "After being with these people like this there is no way you'd get me to go back into committee work. This is real ministry."

Personal agendas of conversion seem to be put aside. People become the focus. People become the subject of evangelization, not its object! Christ resides as the source of the evangelizer's energy. Evangelizers discover a new sense of meaning and purpose for their being in Christ. The church becomes transformed. Indeed the evangelizer receives far more of faith nurturing than s/he ever is able to give. That is the way of true evangelization: we do receive more as we give away that which we have received from Christ.

PART III

THINKING THROUGH THE "WHY" AND "HOW" OF A CARING CHURCH

CHAPTER XIII
MISSIOLOGY: NEW WORD, OLD STORY

I was recently introduced to a church gathering as a "missiologist". The one common feature on the brows of the listeners was puzzlement. At least the word caught their attention. Following my presentation one of my friends commented, "We've sensed a lot of strange things about you over the years, but not that one. What in blazes is a missiologist?" Indeed the term "missiologist" is a newcomer to mainline Christian denominations. I first encountered it in the writings of conservative theologians, then later in the materials coming out of Vatican II. Reformed theologians, somewhere in the middle between Roman Catholicism and the evangelical right, never seemed to use it. At least they didn't until the last few years, when it has become commonly used and understood in ecumenical and evangelical dialogues.

Missiologists are those whose primary concern is the study of the nature and practice of the mission of the church. For them, reaching out to others is front and centre of their work in the life of the church. They may well have an interest in worship and liturgy, an involvement in the nurture and growth of the young and not-so-young. But their primary vocation is in what the church does to the world outside itself. They are essentially outsiders, not insiders. They are world oriented, not church oriented.

Most dictionaries define mission as the act of sending out or being sent out with authority to perform a special duty. In the Christian community, the duty has been to preach, heal, teach and evangelize in the name of the Christ of God.

First, mission is a being sent out. It is from the community within those who gather in the name of Jesus that people are selected to be sent elsewhere. They are challenged to leave the place of their comfort, and go to that place where the community is not. The church is thus the training ground for those who go out in mission. It is the necessary place of nurture and celebration which prepares one for the task. But the church is not the place of mission, primarily. Yes,there are always those within the gathered community who are in continual need of mission and evangelization. There are indeed belongers who are not believers within that community. However, the primary call is to be sent out, to go out. The first word of missiology is go.

Second, the focus of missiologists is on the world, that place out there, or to put it plainly, the many worlds which are not now touched by the Gospel. Hence, their focus is toward understanding the place to which they go. They need to reflect deeply on the nature and condition of men and women who live out there. What are their needs, their questions, their assumptions? What does the Gospel bring — if anything — to that unbelieving forum? What "bridges of God" might be built in the interests of communicating the Christian message and claim? Hence, it becomes "go into the world"... and go with the stances of listening and attending that have been the primary thesis of this book.

The focus of mission in Christ's name therefore is on the needs of the world to which Christ sends us. The place of mission is in that world. The church is the training ground which nurtures and prepares us for the great commission of the One who sends us out, "Go and make disciples." The product we seek is that others, like us, become learners in the way of Christ.

I like to draw the meaning of missiology with two circles. The first is an inward looking circle, like the following:

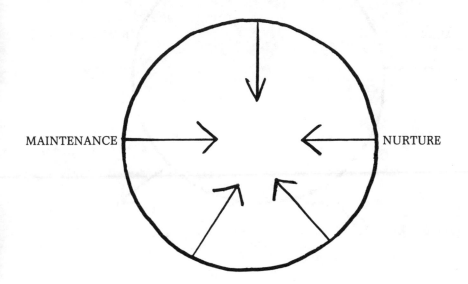

MAINTENANCE   NURTURE

This circle represents the people of God facing inward. They are looking toward each other, as they do in worship, where as they celebrate the story out of which they live and as they help each other grow and mature in the faith through their Christian education programs.

A second circle sees the same persons in the community of faith gathered in a circle, but facing outward. The arrows of their mission intention are focused on the world outside their community, on those who do not celebrate the story they celebrate, who do not live out of its dictates and precepts. They are toward those who choose to march to a different drummer than the God they have experienced in Jesus Christ. They are about mission, or as we shall soon note, evangelization.

So missiology may be a new word, but it is an old story! It is what we have historically done when we have sent missionaries who preach and teach and heal to the farthest ends of the world. We have stood with the oppressed and marginalized in our own country when they have been outside our safe,

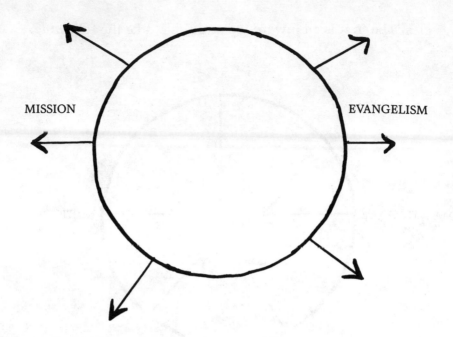

MISSION
EVANGELISM

comfortable, and mostly predictable world, and when their world has not been predictable, comfortable or safe.

CHAPTER XIV
EVANGELIZATION IS NOT
SUCH A DIRTY WORD AFTER ALL

Evangelism has had many practitioners who have dirtied the word. Of course, religion itself has always had many enthusiasts who have made it difficult for others to believe in its credibility and integrity. When the writer was appointed secretary for evangelism of Canada's largest Protestant denomination, many friends and associates were incredulous. They had known me as a jazz musician and co-ordinator of many jazz liturgies, as a social activist and street worker with delinquent youth, as a chaplain and psychologist in a juvenile delinquent training school,as pastor, preacher, and pastoral counsellor. But not as an evangelist. That is because they had not had a chance to struggle with what an evangelist was. They have since struggled with me in reclaiming the name to what it is in the New Testament witness, the task of ordinary Christian folk like you and me. They have even helped us to change the name... just slightly.

The word evangelism comes from the Greek word "euangelion". It is a noun which means simply "the good news". For Christians that means the good news of Jesus the Christ. From this word we also get the word "Gospel". But evangelism is still an "ism". Like many other "isms" it is something we can talk to death and do nothing about. In the history of our mainline churches we have done that well. As one of our critics once said: "I like the way I do my evangelism better than the way you don't do yours."

There is another word in the greek New Testament

which is a little different. It is the verb "euangelizomai". It is an action word which means "to do good news". In translation, it means "evangelization".

It is to the task of evangelization — the doing of the good news — that I would direct our churches, our congregations and the reader. I don't care about all the talk we have evangelism. I do care about our strategies that lead to doing the good news in the global village.

Mission has an object. It is to do justice that others may live more fully. It is to love mercy that we, and others in the global village, may grow toward wholeness. It is to walk humbly with our God so that life may be lived and enjoyed in all its fullness.

Evangelization is about all this, as part of mission, but it is also about something more. It also seeks to engage others with that story which prods us to do justice, gives us the vision to love mercy, and calls us to walk the humble path with our God. Evangelization invites others to be engaged by that story which is the foundation for us, so that they can say "yes" or "no" to that story.

Simply put, evangelism'evangelization is to be the Christian story, to do the Christian story, and to tell the Christian story. It is about three interdependent, interconnected and irrevocably intertwined verbs. One of them cannot be excluded without the whole being lost. All are a necessary part of the task of evangelization.

"Being" evangelism might indicate that all we have to do is to "be" with or for the other person. They will see, or experience, in us the presence of the Christ. Perhaps they will catch the Gospel by osmosis. Such arrogance! Surely our track record of engaging others to Christian commitment that way is evidence enough of its failure.

Social action evangelists sometimes say the importance is in the "doing" of the story. It is matters only that we do justice, stand with the marginalized and speak the prophetic word to the principalities and powers of this brutal godless world. One does not want to underestimate the importance of "doing" Gospel. But to do and to be and not somehow to tell often leaves the hearer/receiver of good news wondering about the "why" of their lives and of your own.

The evangelizer — the good newsperson — is not ashamed to tell the story while doing it and being it. The reluctance of mainline Christians to tell the "why" of their Christian journey is, I feel certain, tied to their fears of being misunderstood. It is not because they do not believe solidly enough or are unwilling to communicate something so central to what makes them Christian and human.

It is easy for us to be the Christian story. We do it readily if telling is also to become part of our life as evangelical Christians, I believe we must recover the biblical understanding of our stories as part of the ongoing story of God. Then we will more easily, and more naturally, tell "who we are and Whose we are".

And then evangelism will cease to be a dirty word. We will not fear to say we are evangelical or evangelists. We will see it as the task of ordinary folk. It will be like when we met Jesus through the eyes of the Samaritan woman, or vice versa. Or like when we saw Philip begin and continue the journey of life with the Ethiopian eunuch.

Or when we become wounded healers to each other!

CHAPTER XV
THE WOUNDED HEALER
AS MATRIX FOR EVANGELIZATION

We come now to identify the ministry of the evangelizer in a particular way, one that may help us to a fuller understanding of evangelization in an holistic way in the decades before us.

The ministry of evangelization needs to be understood as the matrix of being healed and healing the wounds inflicted upon us. Evangelizers recognize themselves as ones who are often being wounded but who are also on the journey of being wounded healers.

Matrix can be defined as the womb. It is that, from which something originates, takes form or direction. The image of the wounded healer is what shapes our model of evangelization. Evangelizers are the already wounded; they are also the wounded healers.

In my research with the church dropouts of Harmony Church, I was beginning to understand a connection between pastoral caring and evangelization. To that point my pastoral caring had been in the liberal tradition. It was not enough. The more I listened to the tapes of my interviews with the dropouts, the more something became clearer: ministry was meaningful *only* when it evolved from the struggles within the ministering person's own life experience. From the ashes of our daily experiences, of hurt and growth comes the salve that can be used to heal another's pain. When identity could be established, honestly and openly, between the healer and the wounded, growth toward faith did happen. When our human stories touched together, even tenuously, evangelization took place. It is was more than pastoral caring; it was faith blooming.

Henri Nouwen's *Wounded Healer*, as I said earlier, is the fundamental model for evangelization today. Nouwen's primary image is that of the wounded Messiah who is the One who is able to liberate humanity from the pain and turmoil of the human journey. He found that image in an old legend in the Talmud, the book of Jewish law. It goes as follows:

Rabbi Yoshua ben Levi came upon Elijah, the prophet, while he was standing at the entrance of Rabbi Simeron Ben Yohai's cave. He asked Elijah, "When will the Messiah come?" Elijah replied:

"Go and ask him yourself."

"Where is he?"

"Sitting at the gates of the city."

"How shall I know him?"

"He is sitting among the poor covered with wounds. The others unbind their wounds all at the same time and then bind them up again. But he unbinds one at a time and binds it up again, saying to himself, 'Perhaps I shall be needed: if so I must always be ready so as not to delay for a moment.'"

Nouwen continues: "The Messiah, the story tells us, is sitting among the poor, binding his wounds one at a time, waiting for the moment when he will be needed. So it is with the ministry. Since it is is their task to make visible the first vestiges of liberation for others, he must bind his own wounds carefully in anticipation of the moment when he will be needed. He is called to be the wounded healer, the one who must look after his own wounds but at the same time be prepared to heal the wounds of others. He is both the wounded minister and the healing minister." (9)

I read on for a bit, and then put the book aside. My mind was flooded with the many scenes of my recent conversations. There had been a bend in the conversational road with Marlene. Why? Things had dramatically changed in the lives of the Banyons. Could I touch the moment when that change began? And what about Philip and the Ethiopian eunuch? Was there something in that story to be recaptured? And Jesus with the Samaritan woman? Any speculations about that part of the Christian story? What about my own story?

I remembered the icy stormy night when I stood in the hospital parking lot after the death of our baby. God has long forgiven me for my curses. It took a long time, and one good friend, to get rid of all that anger and bitterness and to resume my faith journey.

I knew my brokenness, my woundedness. It was painful. I had to undertake the task of binding my wounds one at a time before I could become a wounded healer for others. But that time would come.

My mind then travelled on to Marlene. She touched the scar tissue of my woundedness when she prodded me. "I don't sense that your life has been all sweetness and roses either." She was right. We unravelled my life as we unravelled hers. Life's real and deep moments touched each other. And Marlene again dared to believe, or tried to.

When Karen Banyon touched my woundedness almost brutally, she was asking if there was salve in my life's healed brokenness which might be healing for her. "Is it true that you also lost a son?" And we both grew through sharing.

There were others among the dropouts with whom I shared. Not much seemed to happen for them. Why? Perhaps our stories were too different, could not touch, could not be healing grace for each other.

Yes, the Wounded Healer of Henri Nouwen presented a new and creative image for the recovery of evangelization. It is true that our service as evangelizers will not be authentic unless it comes from a heart and a life wounded by the suffering of which it speaks. It is true that our own wounds can become sources of healing for others along life's wounded way. But that can happen only if those wounds of ours have been healed by the grace of God. It cannot happen if they still bear the poison of the past. These are infectious, not healing wounds.

Why should we wonder about the validity of this new model for evangelism? After all, it is said of the Messiah that "he was wounded for our transgressions; he was bruised for our iniquities." Someone also said of him that "by his wounds are you healed". We know that to be true of Jesus whom we dare to call the Christ! So what of those who are called to be evangelizers in the Body of Christ? It is true also for those in Christ that others are healed by our wounds. Or can be!

CHAPTER XVI
FOR THE WHOLE PEOPLE OF GOD:
ON BEING A ROYAL PRIESTHOOD

I have long been a non-sacramentalist. As clergy of a Reformed church, I had to celebrate the Lord's Supper at least four times each year. For me, it was a memorial feast rather than a celebration.

Then it changed for me, suddenly, almost like a conversion. I was behind the table. It was Communion Sunday. There, sitting in the 13th row from the back on the left side of the sanctuary, were the Banyons. They had been back for about two months. We had shared our woundedness through so many painfilled conversations. Finally we had been victorious in knowing the laughter and joy of the Good News. Karen and Lloyd caught my eye as I was raising the bread to break. As I said, "This is the body of Christ broken for you," I saw their faces clearly through the cleavage in the broken loaf. "My God," I thought, "this loaf is not only about the broken body of the Christ. It is also about the brokenness of Karen and Lloyd. It is their brokenness that we celebrate here also... and my brokenness. It is a sharing in the Bread of Life which is the symbol for all life's brokenness."

Word and sacrament found a new meaning for me. I knew we were all invited guests at a feast in honour of the Christ who shared our brokenness, who said it was all right to be broken... to be healed... to be broken and to be healed again. I was invited to the feast of the community of the walking wounded.

In the sacrament of Holy Communion, we share solidarity with all the wounded children of God. There is nothing awesome about it. It is a recognition of the commonness of our humanity which is a journey toward and through brokennness. My woundedness, which is healed by God's grace, is welcome at the table no matter how apparent its scar tissue (or even how repulsive its memories). So is that of my neighbour and friend whose breaking points have been different from mine. We are all invited guests of the Wounded Healer. We are all rightful participants in the community of the walking wounded.

Why? Because our wounds-healed-by-God's-grace are our identification cards in that community of the walking wounded. We are part of what Peter called "a chosen race, a royal priesthood, a holy nation, God's own people, that you may declare the wonderful deeds of him who called you out of darkness into his marvellous light." (10) It is a priesthood that is the domain of both clergy and lay persons. In it we are called to be priests to each other.

Perhaps a story out of my continuing experience will illustrate best this royal priesthood, the community of the walking wounded.

It was late one evening when the phone rang. I did not recognize the voice on the other end. A man said simply, "My name is Lloyd. I am wondering if you would come over and spend an evening with my family and me. We need someone to talk to. You may know me as the father of Phillip."

That name Phillip was all it took. "Yes, I'll come over tomorrow night about eight." I knew it would be one of those long and painful nights in ministry which I have come to dread, yet love in a deep spiritual sense.

Phillip was a nine-year-old who had been killed on the railroad trestle on the Good Friday, three weeks earlier. I had waited, wondering if we might be asked to take the funeral at Harmony Church. We were not and I was quietly grateful. For me it is still deeply painful to take the funeral of a child , to see a small white coffin, and to enter into the pain and struggle of a family grieving for a child. It re-engages my own struggle every time. Yet I know it to be an area of ministry in which I can be uniquely helpful for I have come to accept my ministry as a wounded healer.

Phillip's family had just moved to our community and

appropriately they asked their former pastor to take the service. However, they had been to Harmony Church twice and sensed something different about it. So they chanced an invitation to a pastor to whom they had only said hello at the church door.

They welcomed me warmly, yet tentatively, into their home. They wanted to talk about Phillip and their grief, and yet they didn't. It was a long evening. They could not believe this could ever have happened. They wept about a happy boy who would never burst through their door again. And God was asked a pile of questions, by them and by me. Not many answers came, because there were no answers.

As our conversation meandered over their last three weeks of grief, it seemed appropriate to share my own story. "I want you to know that I have some sense of what you are going through. We lost a child at birth about seven years ago." No two human journeys are ever quite alike. Yet there are some parallel paths and some points where stories may touch in a helpful way... and so I mentioned my personal history, as a fact, for what help it might be.

I want to footnote something here: It is never helpful to say "I know just how you feel." It is one of the most uncaring, untrue and ultimately unhelpful comments that the evangelist-healer can ever use. The grieving persons want to believe that there has never been a grief like theirs, and indeed there never has been... for them. They need to be permitted their individuality and uniqueness. It is also true that we can never quite get inside another person and understand their journey fully. Let us not try to simplify life or be flippant by saying "I know how you feel" when we never can. Let us rather cherish (yet try to understand) each journey as lived uniquely under God.

Lloyd invited me to come back. So we arranged to talk more the following week. We did so for 13 consecutive weeks, one evening each week. Sometimes they were short conversations of an hour. Some went into the late night and lasted over three hours. Always there were tears, sometimes laughter. Always there were questions, and increasingly some answers. How does one continue to live, or want to live, when life has been so terribly ruptured? Sometimes there was guilt. Often there was anger... at God, at me, at themselves, at their deceased son, at life in general. But always there were moments of common acknowledgement. Indeed it was a mutual journey.

Later there was daylight. It took 13 weeks of mutual discovering before life felt anywhere near whole again. Months and years later we still share some of those same painful thoughts. We have been and still are wounded healers to each other.

So you ask the question, was it worth it? Thirteen weeks, one evening each week, is a lot of pastoral time to invest. Is it time invested appropriately? Unequivocally, I have to say it is! It matters not the result. The wounded healer is always bandaging his/her wounds waiting for the time to unwind those bandages in becoming helpful to another. It is important for wounded healers to unbind those wounds for their own continuing salvation and wholeness, as much as it is important for the grace of healing they may be to another in time of need. Wholeness is a giving and a receiving in the wounded healer ministry!

In the case of Lloyd, the story has continued. Not all do, nor should we expect them to. Our call is merely to faithfulness in the vision of ministry given to us. Some weeks ago I had another phone call. This time I knew instantly who it was. "Guess what I'm up to on Sunday morning?" I chuckled and he continued. "You got it. I'm leading the service at the hospital chapel again. It's tough, preaching to eight people all of whom are in wheel chairs or on hospital beds. You have it easy in those cushy churches. Anyway, thanks to you, that's where I'll be on Sunday."

"And Lloyd, I thank God that you — yes, you — are the one who is going to be there. I thank God because of what you have been through and what you can give to these people."

Indeed I am grateful to God for Lloyd, for his friendship, for his being a wounded healer to me in my own struggles, for his ongoing creative ministry as a wounded healer in the Harmony congregation, and in the business world where he witnesses.

Who do you suspect can best be in ministry to a family who lost a child to crib death last week? Whose life has parallels to that of the family whose daughter drowned in a boating accident last summer at the cottage? Lloyd becomes case-in-point and exhibit A for my thesis: the future of the church as evangelist lies in its ability to become the community of the walking wounded.

The community of the walking wounded includes those who recognize the sufferings of this particular time as their own suffering responsibility and recognize those suffering points as the starting points of their wounded healer ministry. In the 25th chapter of Matthew's Gospel lies, for me, the most troublesome and frustrating of the parables Jesus tells, that of the Last Judgment. We can clearly identify the focus of his — and our — intentional ministry in the faces of the poor, the imprisoned, the marginalized and so on. We are told that in the faces of these is the face of the Christ, there we shall we meet him. Yet we seldom focus on a single verb in that text which unlocks the possibility for our meeting the Christ there. It is the verb see. "Lord, when did we see thee... or see thee not." The more one enters into the ministry of the wounded healer, the more it becomes clear that only the once-wounded have the "eyes to see" those who are now wounded. Strange, yet true, that our brokenness gives us, first, the gift of sight, and later insight! Lloyd sees in the death of a child something unique of both brokenness and opportunity for ministry.

Lloyd's ministry began simply. He was the wounded person who was helped to bind up his wounds and those of his family. He worked at that binding for some months, even years. But then came the invitation, from the one who had been his wounded healer. "Lloyd, I need your help." And we made our first journey into that territory which would always be painful for him (and for me). We went to visit a family who had just lost a child. It was a difficult first experience for Lloyd. He listened. He cried. He told a bit of his story. He came back to visit the Smiths later. He stayed with them through the grief that followed.

So began the ministry of the Wounded Healer at Harmony Church. Soon Lloyd was not alone, however, for Shirley joined him.

Shirley and Ken had been a close couple for 52 years. And then Ken was gone, suddenly and peacefully in the middle of the night. I took his funeral. I remember her words by the graveside, "What do I do now?" I didn't know, but later she would discover the answer for herself.

The first Sunday she came back to church I sat with her during the early moments of worship, while lay people led the opening of the liturgy, as they often did. She had talked about how rough it would be to be there the first time without Ken. Quietly, we slipped into our "widows' row" — an affectionate term used by the inhabitants for their particular mini-church of like-experienced folk — and when it was time for me to take part in the liturgy she simply squeezed my hand and said "thanks". Shirley had made her place in a particular mini-church within the community of the walking wounded. She is still part of it.

Some six months later Shirley called. A bit edgy, I thought, and I was right. She said that she wanted to be doing something more. She felt she had more to give to life, or to the church, and after all, her 72 years should count for something. She wanted the church and life to demand more from her. Later that week she was to find her first new focus for ministry in the community of the walking wounded.

Bill had died. Shirley knew Doris slightly. I told her I would pick her up at and we would go to the funeral parlour together. She was hesitant, but knew she had to do it. The wounded healer met the newly-wounded. Over the weeks ahead Shirley would unbind the wounds of her life's journey and help Doris to begin the binding of her own wounds. Then Doris might be ready when she might be needed in ministry to others... inside the church or outside it.

Imagine a church... I dream of such a church... which begins to recognize its wounded people, whose brokenness has been healed by God's grace. Envision that church becoming intent upon using those healed wounds as salve for ministry to those inside and outside the church. This will be the community of the walking wounded.

Who are these walking wounded? They are the Lloyds and Shirleys and Dorises who have been through life's breaking moments. They have lost a child, or spouse, or parent, or friend; they have lost jobs, or visions, or dreams; they have been handicapped, either by circumstance or birth. Among them are the divorced, the separated, the single parents, and those who have suffered emotional breakdowns. What about those who have been through the turbulent experience of teen-aged revolts, delinquent sons or daughters, alcoholics or the family of alcoholics? The team of the walking wounded thus begins to grow into a community which is large and strong in any congregation. It is the most significant team for ministry, inside and outside the church, if we have the eyes to see them and the ears to listen to their stories. It will also require our patience to train them in this intentional ministry.

Of this, however, I remain convinced: this community of the walking wounded is the matrix — the nurturing place — for the renewal of the church through evangelization. It will not create the dramatic growth claimed by many so-called experts in the church growth field. But it will be a steady and faithful growth in keeping with the Gospel mandate to make disciple/learners who walk in the Way of the Christ.

Key participants in this community of the walking wounded will be those who are on the outside looking in. Those who have dropped out of the community of faith, those who have been broken by life and left the church, are the most fit and eager to the reach out to those who are still on the outside. They have a sharpened sense of what it means to live out there. They have a unique appreciation of what it means to move back into life in the community. They also have the enthusiasm — which is a translation of what it means to be filled with the Spirit — to bring the Christian story as light and liberation to those who are suffering alone.

Church dropouts who have dropped back in must indeed be the core of the community of the walking wounded. Unless one knows one's brokenness, recognizes the pain of being human, knows the reality of one's sin or being sinned against, then one simply does not have the qualifications to be a part of the community of the walking wounded. Life is indeed the school of hard knocks; the church can serve as the hostel of God's healing grace and also as the power plant that makes it possible for the wounded to go back into the fray as wounded healers. One also needs to know the gift of salvation, of healing and wholeness, if one is to be a member of the community of the walking wounded.

How does one begin to develop such a community? By

keeping eyes open to the needs of persons in one's pastoral ministry, so one can recognize the gift in the wound that has been healed. (I did not say recognizing the wound as a gift — that indeed is heresy.) The pastor or caregiver must also help the wounded person to begin to recognize that healed wound as something claimed by God for ministry within the whole people of God. It is sometimes difficult, but needful, to help others accept that they have something to offer in the leadership of the community. This is particularly true if that wound is something despised by the wisdom of this world (but cherished by God).

We have called this group a community. It needs to be a community. People are built for community. Companionship is one of the unique opportunities the church offers in our individualistic, fragmenting world. It begins, however, as a community of two. The wounded healer — the one — begins the process of unbinding her/his wounds with the newly wounded — the second — and they become a twosome on the journey, like Philip and the Ethiopian when the latter invites him to join the chariot pilgrimage. Later, however, one must be introduced to the larger community. The twosome must become a foursome, a group of eight and so on. I have a dream that someday, somewhere, a whole congregation may catch the vision, pay the price of recognition, and become a total community of the walking wounded. It is my dream of what Harmony Church could become!

The small community of walking wounded must also become public. It is not a secret society, hidden in some select pew. It must be visible and owned by the congregation or else its ministry will not be perceived to be real ministry. Visibility begins in the Sunday morning worship. There needs to be a balance of lay and clergy leadership, and these persons need to be those who are identified for this ministry of caring and evangelization. So they give leadership, each and every Sunday, in the prayers and readings and telling of the mission of the church in the world. On a regular basis they give the sermon while the pastor may do some small section in the worship. Surely if we expect the pastor to be able to preach 40 to 52 sermons each year, every lay person has one sermon per year based on their living and breathing for Christ.

There is one stumbling block to all this possibility of lay ministry. You guessed it... the pastor! If this community of the walking wounded is to be mobilized for ministry, the pastor must get out of the way and let the people of God go forward. Too many clergy are the "I'll do it for you" kind of leaders. Often that will get the job done. However, it robs the whole people of God of their rightful role. It negates the priesthood of all believers, that great Protestant principle which we only half believe. It underlines the fact that we are not all really in ministry. So, for Christ's sake (and I use the term advisedly), members of the order of ministry must get out of the way and let the people of God go forward. Then watch the church become what it can become under Christ.

CHAPTER XVII
THE RING OF CARE —
LIKE THE ONE ON YOUR BATHTUB

My daughter and I had been horseback riding. She had been on board a rather difficult beast. In the end, it had dumped her in the dirt. When we came home, she was a mess. Into the tub she would have to go. After a good soaking in her favourite bath bubbles, she came out smelling a bit nicer than the barnyard, and looking a a good deal better. Then I made the mistake of going into the bathroom... and what a mess! The ring around the bathtub was immensely black and gummy. Where she had been was clearly etched for all to see.

The ring of care ought to be etched on the life of the church... like that bathtub ring... so it is clearly visible to all. Particularly to those who need the ring of care: the pain-filled, the broken, the wounded, the church dropout. The trouble is that we mainline Christians have so thoroughly scoured the tub of all its caring evidence that those on the outside looking in do not believe they will find caring within our fellowship. And the truth is, more often than not, they are correct!

Lyla — we met her some chapters ago — came to the church looking for meaning and purpose during the turmoil of putting her life back together as a single parent. Yet she could not break in. They left her on the outside looking in because her story was different from their stories. The church people would not, or could not, be wounded healers to her. Thank God, she had the good sense to look to another congregation. There she found some wounded healers who could share her tears and guilt, unbind their wounds and bind up hers. Today she is significant in her leadership in the church. Regularly she unbinds her wounds in the service of healing others. Like others who have been broken, and healed by God's grace, she has not forgotten the gift of God that other wounded healers have been to her Christian journey of becoming.

What might a congregation look like where the ring of care is obvious? First, it will be a congregation where the welcome mat is just messy enough to be homey and inviting, a clear statement that there is room for some other people in the often closed-groupness of our churches.

A publication of the church growth movement for two decades has been talking about such factors as dynamic pulpit leadership, enthusiastic lay leadership, large parking lots that say there is room for you, lively worship, good music, a homogeneous makeup to the congregation. One writer now says that all these may well be necessary; however, there is one overriding factor which determines whether a church will grow. That factor is whether people in that congregation feel loved. If they feel affirmed and wanted, they will stay: if not they will leave.

Most congregations are tough to break in to, however! In one section of our country they say, smilingly, that when you have lived in that community for 20 years people may begin to think you are one of them. Most of our congregations, as I have experienced them as a visitor, are closed circles, facing inwards, bent on their own agendas. They fail to recognize the stranger in their midst who is looking at that inward circle longing for some involvement. If you doubt this, visit a half dozen congregations where you are not known. Count how many people say hello and ask about you. Sign the guest book and wait for the numerous letters you won't receive, or calls inquiring whether they might be helpful. And if you really want to rough it, go to the coffee hour after the service — most churches have them but the welcome mat is scrubbed so clean you don't dare step on it — and see how included you might be in the conversational circles of strangers. These strangers, if they knew themselves to be wounded healers, would seek you out to become friends!

Let me tell you of one strange, strange church! It happens to know what it is doing. It has a messy welcome mat that is inviting.

I appeared at the church door with my family. A middle-aged woman said hello and then had the audacity to ask, "Is this your first time in our church?" I nodded. She went on. "We're glad you came. Would you come with me and sign our guest book?" A bit reluctantly I went. Another woman came to my wife. In about three minutes she told her all about that congregation and what it had for a family like ours. She pointed out that there were lots of things they could be doing better, but they were struggling to be faithful. When I returned, she asked if she might take the family to a pew. Then she asked if she might take us as her guest to the coffee hour afterward. Now, how do you turn down such an invitation?

After the service and coffee hour we said hello to the pastor. Later that week we got a letter from him. Sure, it was a form letter, personalized by a computer; nonetheless, they had noticed we were there. It was addressed to "Gord and family", the titles Mr. and Mrs. had been scratched out. That was indeed enough to say that we were wanted and invited back.

Some months later I talked to leaders in that congregation. I asked about this intentional welcome mat. They were surprised that I called it "intentional". Apparently it had just evolved because this congregation really does want new folk. They want them to be included. They want their gifts to be used in ministry.

It is a strange church! There are not many around like it. But I am sure that others are beginning to catch the vision about inclusion of the stranger.

A second characteristic of an ideal congregation is that its worship services must show "the ring of care" in an obvious way. Often its worship is less formal than most services in the Reformed tradition. Everything doesn't have to go according to order all the time. On occasion the Spirit is allowed to break through.

Worship which is freeing and caring will most often be for the whole people of God, young and old. Children are welcome participants. Sometimes that means that strange — and wonderful — things will happen. One Sunday at Harmony some 100 youngsters gathered around the font during a baptism. After the sacrament was over, we talked about what had happened. One cute little chap wanted to have a look into the font. I picked him up. He looked in and then started to ask questions. He was heard clearly over the sound system via the neck microphone I was wearing. For 15 minutes he asked questions and I answered. "What do you use the water for? It's kind of messy, eh? Why did these Moms and Dads do this? Did my Mom and Dad ever do that?" And, yes, his mother and father had had him baptized about four years before. So we talked about why I thought they might have done it. Jeremy preached the sermon that Sunday morning, or at least set its framework. It wasn't planned that way but it was a not-soon-to-be-forgotten experience of worship for the whole congregation.

Worship also had a strange opening at Harmony. One of our members was a 30-year-old severely intellectually hand-icapped woman. She was a sister of one of the church dropouts who had dropped back in. She caught the vision of that church through young eyes, and having seen people and pastor exchanging hugs, she felt that worship should not begin before she gave the pastor, or worship leader, a hug. So every Sunday, as worship began, she would make her way to the centre aisle, wrap her arms around the pastor. Harmony folk became accustomed to Brenda's opening of worship and they missed it immensely when she died at age 32. Her funeral was one of the greatest outpourings of love and caring that I have ever witnessed. One of the little people of this world had been a wounded healer to our community.

Our quiet before worship is like a funeral pall to the stranger who comes in search of meaning. Our daring to be human, to say hello to that stranger, to make a few joyful noises to the Lord and to each other sets the tone for a worship which is welcoming and engaging.

Because our worship in the Reformed tradition is so centered on preaching, a third characteristic needs to be identified. Preaching which is simply exegetical or biblical will not touch the lives of those who are on the outside looking in. When they step back inside they will hear strange words, meet stories they do not understand, even see symbols and actions which are not part of their experience. Catholics who have

125

returned after Vatican II often witness to the culture shock of their new church.

Preaching which does not connect the Bible story to the preacher's story and to my story will inevitably fall on deaf ears. For the Word to be heard there must be connecting points between faith and culture, religion and world, Sunday and Monday. For me, the new school of preaching called narrative preaching is preaching at its best. It enables *the* story to be experienced in the context of *our* stories.

The fourth component of this caring kind of congregation is the focus on a caregiving-evangelization ministry. I am convinced that every congregation has a filter through which it looks at ministry. It is helpful if they are clear about what it is, though most have never tried intentionally to identify it. For me, I see the total ministry of the congregation through the filter of evangelization. Our focus is on the circle of God's people facing outward to the world outside the church. Hence our worship, preaching, stewardship and caring are pointing toward the edges of the church's life. Such a congregation is mission focused, not maintenance oriented! It is evangelization oriented, not nurture centred! Or rather, our nurture and worship are directed to the task of empowering people to be in the world, not in the church.

This congregation, then, is one which provides multiple opportunities for people to feel cared for. It also gives people many and varied opportunities to exercise their need to care for others. People who feel cared for by the people of God inevitably soon express the desire to be part of caring for others. That is the contagious congregation! You catch faith like the common cold, by being in contact with people of faith. You catch love by being embraced by those who love. And love and faith, when caught, have to be given away.

The ring of care must be seen and felt primarily in the way we care for people. If we are content to let the pastor or professional staff be the caregivers, our congregation is headed for destruction. If we call elder's visits, which merely pass out communion tokens, caring in the name of the church, then forget it! I know of some elders who even visit by mail! But if these same elders go equipped with the desire to struggle with people's stories as disciples, and stay long enough to help themselves and others in the process of becoming Christian, then theirs is a church that has a renewed sense of the caring ministry.

I remember confessing to my own pastor once that I thought the elder's visit was an absolute waste of time, mine and his. He asked why. I told him. My elder, nice gentleman, would come to the door, hand me my communion cards, all the while leaning out toward the road where his car was. Every time I asked if he would like to come in, he told me how busy he was. "Perhaps some other time"..... but that other time did not come.

I suspect my pastor thought he would teach me a lesson. "I'm going to change your elder, Gord. She's a young teacher... she's the best I've got." And she was. About ten like her in any congregation and you have a really empowered church. She would come to the door, smiling, and as the door opened she invited herself in. She often forgot to give us the cards she came diligently to bring. Small wonder, for she was so intent on discovering what was happening in our lives as Christians and people. Our conversations usually lasted for a couple of hours. She didn't hesitate to pray with us. And she always left us feeling that we still had lots to do for Christ and the church that we were not doing. She also made us feel that we had been strengthened to do it.

Then there are the church dropouts and those on the fringe. We need to see them within that ring of care. Hence, our strategies must include a wounded healer team which can be directed, as opportunity affords, to those for whom we can become ministers of the Christ. It means we must be sensitive to those many opportunities available to us through ministry in the hospital, at funerals, weddings and baptisms. We need to become aware also of our social circles where God has already given us bridges over which we can choose to reach out to minister to others. Our call is to care enough for those who are on the outside looking in. The care-ring must be constantly expanding.

And finally a word about gift discernment. It is a term which has often caused negative responses among mainline missiologists. Perhaps because it has been used almost exclusively by those on the evangelical right. However, of late I have come to embrace the term with a newly found afffection. It has a strange kinship to the ministry of the wounded healer.

This term has generally been used to connote that function in ministry of identifying the natural gifts which God has given each member of the Body of Christ and which are then rightfully called forth in the service of the community. One has the gift of evangelism; another has the gift of healing; someone else has the gift of speaking in tongues; another to interpret those signs. The church calls forth those gifts, identifies them, and claims them for the use of the community.

The congregation which focuses on the ministry of evangelization, through the healed wounds of its people, needs to be clear about two things. It must identify the needs of those in its community. This is always an ongoing process of facing up to what God might be calling the community to be, given its situation in ministry. Second, it needs to be continually identifying the life experiences of its people which can be in service to that community. What has happened, or is happening, to its people that might become the salve of the Gospel to those needs of their extended community? How can they mobilize those life experiences in order that the community may more fully be the Christian story, do the Christian story, and tell the Christian story?

It was clear where my daughter had been. The ring on the bathtub told the story, clear and decisively. So it must be for the church which would be evangelical in this time. The ring of care must be evident. It must be seen. It must be smelled. It must be able to be felt. The ring of care is contagious, if we let it touch the lives of those outside. It invites people on the outside looking in to feel it is worthwhile being on the inside looking out. People want to be cared for and to care for others; hence the evangelical mandate of the church may be fulfilled!

CHAPTER XVIII
P.S.: THANKS FOR THE JOURNEY, GOD!

A decade ago I would have been a reluctant evangelist. I would not have used the term evangelist or evangelization to describe my view of ministry. No way! Today, however, I would use those terms to denote the filter through which I see the totality of ministry. Conversion does happen within God's people. We are not only born again, but again and again as God choses to unfold the mystery of the christian journey to us.

Why this change? I count myself singularly fortunate to have had Seward Hiltner intersect my christian and intellectuial journey. He, more than any other person, pushed me toward the evangelism focus. Today, as the evangelism executive for Canada's largest Protestant denomination, I know I would not be who I am today if our lives had not bumped up against each other, if our stories had not touched and something more of the faithing journey happened for me because of it.

I had asked for Seward as my thesis advisor at Princeton since he had been the one who prodded me into doctoral pursuit in the first place. I was delighted when he said "yes" but was warned that he had only three years until retirement. I had chosen him because I was interested solely in the area of pastoral counselling. And after all, Hiltner was considered one of the foremost in the field of pastoral care, and the father of the clinical pastoral education movement. To this point, I had fancied myself as something of a preacher and pretty good in the pastoral care field. My patron saints in ministry had always been Harry Emmerson Fosdick of the Riverside Church in New York City and Norman Rawson of St James United Church in Montreal. I had entered ministry largely because of the latter's influence on my life while in the business community in Montreal. So, a degree in pastoral counselling with Hiltner's signature on it would really help me up the pastoral ladder...or so I thought!

I was to be surprised by God again! This man Hiltner would put my whole ministry career on a new trajectory. We talked our way through the thesis project. I told him how I wanted to use the church dropout population of the Harmony congregation to better understand the nature of pastoral conversation. That was a term first coined by Heije Faber of Holland. He listened long to the draft proposals. Then he mused quietly. "Then what you are really after is trying to understand the interconnection between pastoral care and evangelism." I was shocked, and not the least amused. I didn't want to be about evangelism, and I didn't expect to hear him use that word. After all he was a liberal of the liberals. In his writings I had not discovered an author who was concerned about faith gains. But then, one's books don't always tell about the whole person.

I did not know the stuggling Hiltner; never had I been introduced to the brokenness of this man's journey. I would soon learn that the greatness of the pastoral counsellor came from his indepth understanding of the humanity of personhood. His title at Princeton, Professor of Theology and Personality, was more than a title; it was a definition of the man! I would see his tears; I would hear his laughter; and I would feel his anger, when he felt I could do better. He would made me mad and glad and sad, but he helped me to become a better human. He turned a reluctant evangelist into one for whom the journey of evangelizer is indeed "good news". "Euangelizomai" — to do Good News — is what ministry has totally become for me.

Perhaps, it sounds a bit too much glory posthumously to an academic. I am grateful to Seward. But I am most grateful to God for causing our paths to cross. It was one of those God occasions which happened not because of anything I did or achieved. After all, I did earlier affirm that "what I am now is where I was when". One of Seward's final books called "Theological Dynamics" contains a chapter titled "Grace and Grat-itude". The divine action is "grace" to which the appropriate human reaction can only be "gratitude". My life has been uniquely graced by God, even on the slippery slopes and dark-ened valleys. And so I can merely say, thanks for the journey, God!

Thanks for the journey, God, which has taught me that all ministry ought to be seen through the filter of those on the outside looking in. Evangelization is where it is at.

Thanks for the journey, God, that has helped me recog-nize my own brokenness. To know that it can, and will, be healed in that community which lifts the loaf of the bread of brokenness and shares the cup of the new wine of the kingdom.

Thanks for the invitation to be part of that Shalom kingdom where people cared enough to help my brokenness, mending it into the firm scar tissue of creative ministry.

Thank you, God, for the journey that caused me to meet Marlene, the Banyons, Shirley, Lloyd, and Lyla. For they have become for me, and with me, partners in the Community of the Walking Wounded.

Thank you, God, for the vision of what that community can become! And will become in churches like Harmony!

REFERENCES

1. Year Book, 1985, The United Church of Canada, Toronto, Canada.

2. Bibby, Reginald: Canadian Commitment, Part One: The Nature of Religious Commitment in Canada, The United Church of Canada, 1979.

3. Savage, John S., The Apathetic and Bored Church Member, Lead Consultants, Pittsford, New York, 1976.

4. Bibby, Reginald: Anglitrends, Toronto, Canada, 1986.

5. The Unchurched American, The Princeton Religion Research Center and The Gallup Organization, Inc., 1978.

6. Sadaka, Neil, Sadaka's Back, Polydor Records, 1974.

7. Clinebell, Howard J. Jr., Basic Types of Pastoral Counselling, Abingdon Press, Nashville, 1966.

8. Hiltner, Seward, Ferment in the Ministry, Abingdon Press, Nashville, 1969

9. Nouwen, Henri J.M., The Wounded Healer, Doubleday and Company, Inc., Garden City, New York, 1972.

10. I Peter 2:9, Revised Standard Version, Holy Bible.

NOTES

NOTES

NOTES